Hiring Smart for

Competitive Advantage

The Results-Driven Manager Series

The Results-Driven Manager series collects timely articles from *Harvard Management Update, Harvard Management Communication Letter,* and the *Balanced Scorecard Report* to help senior to middle managers sharpen their skills, increase their effectiveness, and gain a competitive edge. Presented in a concise, accessible format to save managers valuable time, these books offer authoritative insights and techniques for improving job performance and achieving immediate results.

Other books in the series:

A Timesaving Guide

THE RESULTS-DRIVEN MANAGER

Hiring Smart for Competitive Advantage

• • •

Harvard Business School Press

Boston, Massachusetts

Library of Congress Cataloging-in-Publication Data

Hiring smart for competitive advantage.
    p. cm. — (The results-driven manager series)
    ISBN 1-59139-972-6
    1. Employee selection. 2. Employment interviewing. 3. Employees—
Recruiting. I. Harvard Business School Press. II. Series.
    HF5549.5.S38H573 2005
    658.3'11—dc22

                                                      2005018861

Contents

Contents

Assess Candidates' Cultural Fit

Tap the Right Talent Pools

Contents

Use the Internet to Recruit

Use the Internet to Recruit

Introduction

. . .

What's the *most* valuable action you can take to help ensure your company's success? Hire the right people. When you select the best possible candidates to serve as individual contributors on your team, as leaders of your unit or division, or as consultants who will augment your staff temporarily, you generate crucial results for your unit *and* your company. By assembling a top-notch workforce, you enable your organization to:

- Carry out its high-level, competitive strategy

- Drive new growth and capture market share from rivals

- Create innovative products and services

- Seize advantage of changes in the business landscape, such as new technologies and shifting consumer desires

- Smoothly transition new leaders into position as their predecessors retire or rotate into other roles

Clearly, "hiring smart" can give your company a vital edge over rivals—something that's increasingly important in this age of stiffening competition. Equally important, it enables you to build a reputation as a talented manager and advance your own career. Yet just as selecting the right employees has become more crucial, it has also grown more challenging—thanks to profound changes transforming the business landscape.

Hiring Smart: More Important—and Challenging—Than Ever

At all levels in an organization, "hiring smart" has become more crucial *and* complex than ever, for several reasons. First, the knowledge era is here to stay: Whereas companies used to compete on the basis of their physical assets (their factories, equipment, and other tangible resources), they now compete based on their intangible assets—the human beings they employ, and the skills and knowledge those men and women bring to the table. Hiring managers must therefore know precisely what kinds of abilities to look for in job applicants and how to assess candidates' qualifications in new ways.

Second, organizational cultures have undergone major transformation. In many companies, command-and-control hierarchies have given way to entrepreneurial, cross-functional teams in which people must influence others over whom they have no formal authority. These changes call for employees who excel at collaborating and at leveraging informal sources of power, and who relish the high energy and creative exchange of ideas that characterize such teamwork. Thus companies must attract job applicants who possess not only the technical skills required by the work but also the unique (and often hard to find) personality traits that foster a collaborative culture.

Third, the composition of the workforce is also shifting. To respond flexibly to expanding and contracting volumes of work, many companies are augmenting their traditional staff with contingent workers—including consultants. Moreover, in addition to drawing from the usual talent pools to find individual contributors, managers, and executives, organizations are exploring several previously untapped sources of employees—such as persons with disabilities and workers who serve on a contingent basis. Hiring contingent and other nontraditional employees offers companies important advantages. But it also requires managers to master new skills in order to evaluate and select such employees.

Finally, the Internet has opened exciting new channels for finding and screening potential new employees. For hiring managers, that's good news in many respects. For example, the Web vastly increases the pool of applicants you can choose from. However, finding and hiring talent via the Internet also presents some challenges. To illustrate, a manager may mistakenly focus only on "active" candidates (those who post their résumés on online job boards) and neglect to tap the more valuable pool of "passive" candidates (those well-qualified workers happily employed elsewhere).

All of these changes point to the need for managers to approach hiring with an entirely fresh mindset—from defining job qualifications in new ways and reexamining their approach to interviewing, to actively selecting individuals who differ markedly from themselves in personality and strategically using the Internet. On its own, each of these changes poses a tough enough challenge—especially when today's manager already feels buried under mountains of other responsibilities. Put these changes all together, and you might understandably begin to feel overwhelmed!

This volume provides potent guidelines and strategies for navigating the shifting terrain that the hiring process has become. Organized into four parts, the selections within address the major challenges of hiring outlined above. Here's a glimpse at what you'll discover as you work your way through the volume.

Sharpening Your Interviewing Skills

Gone are the days when hiring managers would ask candidates, "Where do you see yourself in five years?" or

"What are your most important strengths and weaknesses?" Today, you need a whole new approach—before, during, and after each job interview—to extract the right kind of information from those hopeful applicants sitting across from you in your office.

Business writer Pierre Mornell opens this section with his article "How to Shift the Burden of Hiring onto the Candidate." According to Mornell, busy managers can reduce the time consumed during the interview process by better preparing for, conducting, and analyzing each job interview.

During the preparation phase, for instance, ask the candidate to submit a cover letter with his or her résumé or to visit your company's Web site and write his or her impressions. Then use the letter or notes to evaluate the person's written communication skills. While interviewing, ask the candidate questions such as "What's the most important thing you contribute to any organization?" "What are three things you like and dislike about your current position?" and "When have you failed, and how did you deal with the experience?" Give the candidate a small post-interview assignment to glean further information about his or her skills.

In "Conducting a Great Job Interview," business writer Michael Hattersley offers additional recommendations. For example, be aware of the "pat" answers to typical interview questions that many candidates prepare. Develop fresh questions to which job seekers can't prepare packaged responses. Also look for red flags while checking references—such as a hesitant tone of voice, or a surprise reaction that the candidate is being considered for this job. In addition, focus on the candidate's track record, asking yourself whether the person has acquired the experience, skills, and technical knowledge you've defined as essential to the job. During the interview, maintain control by ensuring that you—not the candidate—ask all the questions. Listen more than you talk, and be suspicious of a highly polished candidate who displays every possible desired attribute.

In "Use Case Interviewing to Improve Your Hiring," executive coach and organizational development expert Melissa Raffoni shifts the focus from the overall interviewing process to strategies for assessing job candidates' skills. Through case interviewing, you "describe a scenario illustrating a business problem the candidate might encounter on the job." For example, perhaps you "ask the candidate what strategy he or she would use to develop a new business" in your industry, or you present a problem related to launching a new product or turning around a declining business. During the interview, "the candidate is expected to ask a series of questions and ultimately present a solution to the problem."

Case interviewing offers several benefits: It lets you see how an applicant's mind works with little preparation and enables you to gauge his or her strategic thinking, analytic ability, and communication skills. It also gives candidates a better understanding of the job in question.

Just as you need to encourage interviewees to reveal vital information about themselves, you must also convey your managerial abilities during a job interview. By doing so, you help the candidate analyze the potential match and interpersonal "chemistry" that he or she would experience while reporting to you. If an applicant doesn't ask you about such matters during the interview, find a way to convey them yourself.

To that end, "Interviewing Your Prospective Supervisor with Rich Wellins" (senior vice president at Development Dimensions International) outlines specific information to present to interviewees. For example, describe how you help direct reports achieve their professional goals and give examples of techniques you use to encourage better collaboration within your team. Throughout the interview, demonstrate genuine interest in and respect for the candidate by maintaining eye contact, answering questions, and listening thoughtfully.

Understanding what *not* to ask during a job interview is just as important as knowing what to ask. Why? Certain questions are downright illegal and can expose your company to liability in the form of lawsuits ranging from sex, race, and age discrimination to religious and ability discrimination. The article "Don't Ask These Questions! How to Avoid Breaking the Law in a Job Interview" lists the "nine worst questions" to ask during an interview. These include "How old are you?" "Are you married?" "What religious holidays do you observe?" "What is your native language?" "Have you ever been arrested?" and "Do you have any disabilities?"

The safest way to avoid asking the wrong questions is

to check with your human resources or legal department for interviewing guidelines and to understand local, state, and federal anti-discrimination laws.

Assessing Job Candidates' Cultural Fit

As business writer David Stauffer maintains in "Cultural Fit: Why Hiring Good People Is No Longer Good Enough," the definition of what constitutes a "perfect fit" in a job candidate has expanded beyond the attributes and skills listed on the typical résumé. Increasingly, hiring managers must also take into account "softer" characteristics that suggest a candidate's potential to fit into their unit's or company's culture.

Stauffer urges managers to assess job seekers' potential "values match" in addition to the traditional talents-and-responsibilities match. For example, if your organization's ability to implement its innovation strategy hinges on openness to new ideas, no matter who generates them, anyone you hire must demonstrate that same value. Stauffer also recommends clarifying the key behaviors your employees must embody to support the corporate strategy—whether it's always being pleasant to customers, sharing information, or responding flexibly to new challenges.

How to gauge candidates' potential cultural fit? Tests can help, as business writer Edward Prewitt explains in "Personality Tests in Hiring: How to Do It Right."

According to Prewitt, a handful of guidelines can ensure that you get the most useful information from tests. For example, before administering tests, specify the values and behaviors that define your corporate culture. Develop crystal-clear criteria for optimum behavior. Consider hiring a consulting psychologist to determine whether the test you have in mind can target the qualities you're looking for. Moreover, don't rely on tests alone. View test results as "one of three legs on a stool, where the other two [legs] are interviews and the candidate's track record." Also be aware of laws restricting the content of pre-employment tests—such as questions about sexual preference and religious beliefs. Finally, ensure that all test questions have "predictive validity"; that is, they accurately measure the traits you're interested in *and* they predict behavior in the specific job in question.

One cultural characteristic that many companies test for is emotional intelligence (EI). Defined as a set of social and self-management skills, EI can account for 15 to 45 percent of a person's success on the job, according to experts cited in the article "Hiring (Emotionally) Smart." This selection provides recommendations for using a test known as the EQ-i. A self-report instrument, the EQ-i can help you assess potential employees' stress-management style, adaptability, and other EI qualities. Most companies administer the test after a candidate has had an initial interview with the hiring manager and a representative from human resources. The results can point to aspects of the candidate's EI skills that bear further investigation.

But you don't need a test to assess EI, say some experts. If testing seems too involved, conduct "behavioral-event interviewing" instead. For example, ask a candidate to describe a time when she felt frustrated by someone who didn't understand her idea. Listen for how she decoded the reactions of others at the time of the misunderstanding. Can she keep workplace tensions in proper perspective?

To hire people who make the best cultural fit with your unit or company, you may need to select someone who has a temperament vastly different from your own. That's the subject of writer Liz Simpson's article "Managers: To Make a Good Hire, Take a Good Look Inside." According to Simpson, "Managers who give in to the 'just like me' bias, hiring candidates who are almost carbon copies of themselves, are only setting themselves up for failure."

To assemble the right mix of personalities in your team requires self-awareness. Ask trusted colleagues to help you realistically assess your own strengths, weaknesses, and personal style. Ask yourself which needed cultural attributes (such as ability to resolve conflict productively or capacity to generate creative new ideas) are underrepresented in your team and can be filled by new hires. Also develop strategies for handling the inevitable friction that arises when people with contrasting temperaments work together—such as establishing agreed-upon rules for debating ideas during meetings.

In bringing together individuals with different temperaments to form the ideal team, many managers include employees who have a strong entrepreneurial background. According to business editor Kirsten Sandberg in "The Lessons of 'Brand You': Advice for Managing Talent," entrepreneurial types often bring a unique passion and a "take the bull by the horns" mindset to their work—qualities that can generate important benefits for your team.

But some caveats apply, too. For example, look for proof of real staying power, not just a string of isolated successes, in an entrepreneurial candidate's professional background. And ensure that the person embodies the attitudes and behaviors that define the company's culture. For instance, "if someone was born to be wild, identifies with Peter Fonda more than Peter Pan, and can see himself as an easy rider but not as a Mouseketeer, then chances are he belongs at Harley-Davidson, not at Walt Disney."

Tapping the Right Talent Pools

To optimize your unit's or company's workforce, you need to tap all the right talent pools—whether you're searching for just the right leader, consultant, or new hire from a previously overlooked source. The first three selections in this section focus on finding and developing exceptional leaders. In "Do You Know What's in Your Leadership Pipeline?" business writer Stephen Nelson explains how to achieve a leadership-development mindset to ensure a reliable supply of internal talent.

One key: "When you're evaluating job candidates, it's not enough just to ask if a person is qualified for job A. You must also determine whether she can grow and be developed for job B." Then you need to discern who among your current employees or job candidates should refill job A. Another key: "Spell out the leadership needs flowing from each goal on your strategic plan. Then assess how your current leadership pool matches up with those needs. As you move through the year, assess the leadership implications whenever a strategic goal is modified or a new one added."

To evaluate an internal or external candidate's leadership potential, also assess whether he or she has acquired the appropriate "schools of experience." Consultant Scott Anthony and management professor Clayton Christensen turn to this subject in "Which Schools of Experience Should Your Executives Attend?" According to these authors, too many hiring executives overemphasize industry experience while evaluating potential new leaders. Result? The new hire defaults to common industry solutions rather than generating new ideas and strategies.

Instead of industry knowledge, look for experience in solving the unique challenges facing your unit or company. For instance, Levi Strauss hired an executive from a motor-oil maker to help the company start selling jeans to Wal-Mart—a major shift in its strategy. The executive had little knowledge of the apparel business. But in his previous position he had solved challenges related to working with Wal-Mart. Thus, he brought valuable experience to Levi Strauss.

In addition to specific problem-solving experiences, today's leaders must know how to manage large, fluid talent pools comprising contingent workers, consultants, and virtual teams. The article "The War for Managerial Talent" offers suggestions for finding such managers. Your best bet may *not* be to use your company's formal recruiting process. Instead, conduct broader, more imaginative searches beyond the small number of traditional sources (such as the same schools or the same industry). Look for people who have different educational backgrounds and who hail from different industries and countries. And don't wait for active job seekers to find you—during a drum-tight labor market, *you* need to do the hunting. Finally, be willing to bend your compensation policies, if necessary, to attract managers capable of wringing extraordinary performance out of a constantly shifting workforce.

Many companies' workforce-management strategies hinge on hiring consultants to augment their traditional staff. If this describes your organization, you'll need to hone your ability to select and oversee consultants in your unit. In "How to Choose—and Work with—

Consultants," business writer Tom Rodenhauser advises hiring consultants only if you have a clear understanding of the project's mission, your organization fully supports the consultant's mission, the engagement's end date is clear, and your company can provide ongoing support for the project after its completion.

Rodenhauser also lays out a process for finding the right consultant—including using directory companies such as Dun & Bradstreet—and evaluating candidates' project potential. Crucial questions to ask candidates (beyond "What's your fee?") include: "What kinds of assignments have you conducted that are applicable to our current problem?" "What is your understanding of the problem we're trying to solve?" and "Do you guarantee your work?"

In addition to using consultants, numerous organizations are tapping previously overlooked sources of valuable employees. In "Hiring Crunch? Here's an Untapped Labor Pool," William Hargis, Jr., shares his experiences in hiring people with disabilities. A general manager for an industrial laundry company, Hargis took advantage of a federal tax incentive that companies qualify for once someone with disabilities works at the organization 400 hours. "Thanks to the incentives, I could essentially hire two people for one salary," he notes. By matching job responsibilities and equipment to disabled employees' capacities, the company has reduced waste and saved thousands of dollars each month. Moreover, the disabled employees are "never late" and "they work hard"—

two qualities that have improved morale at the company and strengthened the stability of its workforce.

Making Savvy Use of the Internet

To find the right employees, you have numerous traditional strategies at your disposal—including using search firms, placing job postings in newspapers and magazines, and asking current employees for referrals. The Internet offers another avenue through which to get the word out about job openings and attract interested candidates. But though online recruiting and hiring can vastly increase your pool of candidates, it also raises challenges.

In "Online Hiring? Do It Right," you'll find tips for making the most of online recruitment sites. For example, use the Internet to reach "passive" candidates—highly qualified workers who are already happily employed. They make up a larger and more appealing labor pool than "active" candidates, who have posted their résumés on online job boards. To reach passive candidates, dedicate a recruiting team to the task. Have them do demographic studies of the sorts of people you want to hire. Data in hand, they can then go to job-search Web sites frequented by prime candidates.

In "Finding Talent on the Internet," writer Patricia Nakache offers additional advice. For instance, use your company Web site not only to post job openings but also to "market" your organization to prospective employees and to accept job applications. Ensure that the site is easy to use: One company allows candidates to submit their résumés either by filling out an online form or by pasting an existing electronic résumé into the form. Also consider exploring unconventional approaches to Internet recruiting. For example, browse the Usenet—a collection of electronic bulletin boards—to identify forums related to expertise you're seeking. Discussion participants could make good candidates or may have valuable leads to recommend.

Hiring smart is bound to grow even more challenging in the decades ahead, as the pace of change in the business world steadily accelerates. But that doesn't mean you can't continually sharpen your hiring skills. Indeed, you'll *need* to hone those abilities regularly as you progress through your career. To that end, after you've read the selections in this volume, ask yourself these questions:

- "In what respects should I change my approach to interviewing job candidates? How can I better prepare for and conduct interviews, and what questions should I be asking?"

- "What key cultural characteristics must members of my team demonstrate in order to help my company succeed? How can I gauge those characteristics in potential new hires?"

- "What overlooked talent pools should I be tapping in my search for talented employees? How might I select the right consultants for my team? And how can I cultivate leadership 'bench strength' in my unit?"

- "How might I make better use of the Internet to recruit, screen, and hire top-notch employees?"

By regularly pondering such questions, you generate a steady stream of ideas for hiring smart. Your team—and your company—will thank you.

Sharpen Your Interviewing Skills

· · ·

Interviewing job candidates involves far more than merely conducting the interview. You need to apply a whole new approach—before, during, and after each interview—to extract the most valuable information from those hopeful applicants sitting across from you in your office.

The selections that follow lay out powerful techniques for sharpening your interviewing skills. For example, start testing an applicant's communication skills *beforehand,* by asking her to visit your company's Web site and document her impressions. During the interview, pose a troubling scenario to the job seeker—a delayed product launch, for example—and ask him how he'd handle it. You'll gain a sense of his problem-solving skills. After the interview, assign the applicant a small task to glean further information about her abilities.

As you'll discover, it's also vital to convey information about yourself during an interview—such as your approach to helping direct reports develop their careers. And it's crucial to understand which questions to steer clear of—to avoid exposing your company to anti-discrimination lawsuits.

How to Shift the Burden of Hiring onto the Candidate

An Interview with Pierre Mornell

• • •

The first phase of psychiatrist Pierre Mornell's professional life consisted of teaching, providing counseling to individuals, couples, and families, and writing books about relationships in the bedroom. Beginning in 1982, however, he began to shift his focus to the boardroom, consulting to corporations and nonprofit organizations about hiring, executive evaluation, and managing change. He was the first dean of the university faculty for the Young Presidents' Organization, and is an occasional lecturer at the Harvard and Stanford business schools. He spoke with Harvard Management Update about his book, *Hiring Smart!*

Is hiring the right people more important now than it has ever been?

I don't know. But Arthur Rock, who was instrumental in the founding of Intel, Teledyne, and Apple, says you should invest in people, not ideas. It's so basic, yet people tend to forget it, or think it's simple—and it's not. I think it's kind of a dirty little secret: everybody has always known that a company's future is tied to its people, that a company's eventually going to go under if the people aren't right, but few people talk about it.

Your book essentially calls for spending more time on hiring decisions. Aren't most managers already too busy?

Managers need to spend more time initially—and different kinds of time—on hiring matters. But the ultimate goal is to put systems in place that will save the company time as well as money. If you ask a company to diagram its hiring system, very often the result will look like a Rube Goldberg drawing. It needs to be simplified, which is not the same thing as making it simplistic: it's a question of working through the complexities, determining what works and doesn't work for your particular company.

For example, I consulted with American Golf Corporation to help design a system for hiring general managers. The final product was a one-page chart; it looks simple, but it took six months to hammer out. And it met with predictable resistance. Yet I cannot tell you how much time and money it has saved for that organization.

Hiring Smart! describes a different kind of hiring system, one that pays more attention to people's behavior than to their words, one that places less emphasis on the interview and more emphasis on the candidate's track record. The goal is to shift the weight of the 800-pound hiring gorilla from the interviewer to the interviewee.

What do you mean by that?

Many managers hate conducting interviews because they've got so much work to do. But there are strategies you can use, beginning in the pre-interview phase, to shift the burden—that hiring gorilla—onto the candidate. Ask for a cover letter along with the résumé as a means of assessing a candidate's written communication skills. United Electric Controls asks candidates for machinist positions to assess company-supplied blueprints. (The result? Fifty percent don't return the applications!) Or, you might ask applicants to visit one of your stores or Web sites and write up their impressions.

Any other suggestions for the pre-interview phase?

Well, first I think it's worth considering a five-minute telephone screening of applicants. Of course, you've got to have the most intuitive person in the firm doing the screening. If you have the wrong person doing it, all bets are off. The telephone screeners have got to have terrific b.s. detectors. Even then they're going to be fooled sometimes, because there are people that give terrific phone interviews—they're clear, concise, complete, funny, articulate, and also look great on the résumé. But as soon as they walk into the room, you realize you've made a mistake. That's very common. It's why I suggest an initial, or pre-interview, interview, in which you ask selected candidates to come in for 20 minutes, especially if they're local.

Moving to the interview phase ...

Many managers feel tremendous pressure to ask all the right questions—such as, "What are your strengths and weaknesses?" or, "Where do you want to be in five years?" The result is an interview that's boring as sin. Instead, managers should ask the candidate to talk about something that is of interest to him or her or to bring in some work samples. Take six or seven of your favorite questions (the book lists 53 examples). For example, "How are you going to lose money for me?" which is really,

"Where have you made mistakes in the past, and where might you make mistakes in the future?" Give your written questions to the candidate, saying, "Here are the five areas I'm most interested in. I'm going to listen for the next 20 minutes and not interrupt, so take your time." This relieves some of the pressure the interviewer feels to be smart or funny. It also avoids the most common problem in interviews: the interviewer's talking too much.

Are there any secrets to becoming a more adept listener?

I think it's helpful to take notes. But more important, 95% of the people I work with say they fall in love with a candidate even before she sits down; they start selling the company almost before the candidate starts talking. If you're under tremendous pressure to talk about the organization, bite your tongue: hold off until the last five minutes of the interview.

It's amazing to me how most people welcome the chance to talk. When you're listening closely, I think the important themes will come out. For instance, I often interview perfectionists, people who are perfect academically or professionally. I ask myself, "What's on the other side of the looking glass? Where are the imperfections in these people's lives? Where do they let down, how do they deal with stress?" Because that will invariably show up on the job.

Isn't it naive to expect a forthright answer to the question, "How are you going to lose money for the company?" Isn't indirection often the most direct route to the truth?

The most important part of the interview is the relationship you establish. You don't start off with, "How are you going to lose money for me?" I also try to think of *how* somebody answers rather than *what* they answer—the candor instead of just the words. I remember one perfectionist who responded to my probing for imperfections and for how she handled stress by saying,

The Candidate Will Be Here in 20 Minutes— What Should I Ask?

The following are representative interview questions. Always remember that questions must be job related unless the candidate initiates the subject.

- What is the most important thing you contribute to any organization?
- How do you deal with stress or conflict? What are the clues you have come to recognize that signal you are under too much stress?
- What are your favorite books, films, Web sites?
- Name three things you like and dislike about your current position.

"Those are all very good questions a
about them, because you're absolutel
them." She didn't initially answer my
was thoughtful, she knew that we ha
and she conveyed that.

Maybe I'm too cynical, but isn't it rare for candidates to let their guard down like that?

I couldn't agree more. Candidates today are overpro-
grammed, and that's why I deemphasize the interview
itself. An interview tells you about chemistry and about

- When have you failed? Describe the circumstances and how you dealt with and learned from the experience.
- Whom do you turn to for help when making decisions?

Curveballs

- Ask three questions at once. See if the candidate remembers the questions without reminders.
- Give conflicting opinions early in the interview. Then see if the candidate agrees with both opinions throughout the interview.
- Ask, "How are you going to lose money for me?" (The question is really: "Where have you made mistakes before? Where might you make mistakes again?")

---

well somebody interviews; for example, a good con artist can fool me every time. I've been blindsided, in my capacity as a psychiatrist, by alcoholic and drug-addicted lawyers and doctors, who were so convincing that even they didn't know when they were lying.

In addition, today's candidates are very prepared for the dozen most common interview questions. Which is why the 5% to 10% who do respond with great candor go up tremendously in my estimation. It's such a breath of fresh air: suddenly the interview takes on a certain meaningfulness that is not there when the candidate is giving canned answers to standard questions.

Why don't you believe in stress interviews?

Stress puts up walls. Maybe it's okay if you're interviewing a football coach, criminal defense lawyer, or labor negotiator, where stress is going to be part of the job. But the point of most interviews is to take down the walls, so why stress the person?

On the other hand, you need to get a feel for how somebody performs in real-life situations. It's always a question of *what* problems will arise, never *if* problems will arise. If you haven't discovered a problem with a candidate, you're missing something. So always ask what problems are likely to occur, because when they do—whether in six weeks or six months—you'll be better prepared to deal with them.

Mornell's Maxim says, "The best predictor of future behavior is past behavior." The time to find out about the specific problems that come with any candidate is often the postinterview phase, when you're contacting references to learn more about past performance (despite the inherent difficulties in our litigious society). Also, giving the candidate a postinterview assignment—even something as minor as a follow-up phone call—can be useful. By the end of a process in which candidates have had to write a cover letter or perform some pre-interview task, do most of the talking, and attend to some follow-up issues, you will have invariably filtered out those candidates who just aren't motivated or can't perform.

Isn't passion for the job overrated these days?

My secretary used to work for a federal district court judge. The candidates for the clerk positions were the best and the brightest out of the nation's top law schools. Many candidates talked with her before their interview, but then ignored her when they came out of their meeting with the judge. These candidates didn't get the job, because the secretary was a key person. It had nothing to do with passion—the ability to work in a team atmosphere was just as important to a clerk's job as were smarts and the ability to write. Neglecting the secretary was thus a big red flag. With certain jobs there are more important issues than passion—think about editors, mechanics, or programmers. So passion is only part of the 200-piece puzzle that constitutes hiring.

For Further Reading

Hiring Smart! How to Predict Winners and Losers in the Incredibly Expensive People-Reading Game by Pierre Mornell (1998, Ten Speed Press)

Reprint U9808B

Conducting a Great Job Interview

. . .

Michael Hattersley

A number of useful books have been published on what to say when interviewed for a job, but much less attention has been paid to what the interviewer should do. Especially at larger companies with personnel departments or access to recruiters, executives often find themselves at the end of the process, choosing perfunctorily among the two or three candidates presented to them. Since picking the right direct reports can be crucial to an organization's effectiveness, and to a manager's career, this kind of passivity can be a mistake. Managers should take a more active role in the hiring process, beginning with an understanding of the important do's and don'ts in conducting a productive interview.

Preparing for the Interview

First, understand the nature and purpose of the interview. Is this a courtesy interview—for example, one offered to an internal candidate even though he's already been deemed unsuitable for the job? (Such interviews should be kept to a minimum, even though, at times, they're politically necessary.) As a general rule, you should aim to be as frank as you can with the applicant about where he stands. Be prepared to describe the duties of the job and the criteria for selection, explain the hiring process, and define the time line for your decision.

Clarify the drill ahead of time. Does it involve an hour's conversation or a tour of the facility, lunch, and meetings with others? All of this should be clear to the candidate before he arrives.

Be conversant with the applicants' likely strategies. A sophisticated candidate will usually come prepared— by training, experience, and reading—to manage the interview on her own terms. All too many books identify "best" answers to the most asked questions or lay out interview strategies designed to impress a future boss. The future boss needs to be aware of these to recognize— and sometimes counter—them, in order to create a revelatory interview. Some generic themes stand out in the literature for interviewees: Candidates should take control of the interview by asking questions. They should have those prepackaged answers in mind for commonly asked questions. And they should research the company, the position, and the interviewer.

As the interviewer, you should learn as much as possible about the candidate before the interview. This may mean that, after narrowing down the pool, you request and check references before, rather than after, you've decided on a candidate. Too often, managers use references as a confirmation of a judgment already made.

> No candidate should be hired primarily for her interview skills.

If you do check references beforehand, be alert to red flags. Few recommenders will express overt doubts; after all, they've been chosen by the candidate. So watch for more subtle signals: reserved tone, surprise the candidate is being considered for this job, lack of senior or enthusiastic endorsements from the candidate's previous employer.

Clearly, too, the interviewer should know what she's

looking for. In *Interviewing*, a guide sponsored by the *National Business Employment Weekly*, Arlene S. Hirsch advises job candidates that employers are usually seeking the following qualities:

- Show you will fit into the work environment.

- Be likeable.

- Have the skills to do the job.

- Be ready to work hard to pursue the organization's goals.

- Make the employer look good.

In *Power Interviews*, Neil Yeager and Lee Hough tell candidates what they believe interviewers look for most:

- Aggressiveness and enthusiasm

- Communication skills

- Record of success

- Rational thought process

- Maturity

- Planning and organization

- Reaction to pressure

Both books offer specific strategies to convey these qualities through a combination of self-improvement, interview strategy, and choosing the right jobs to pursue. But as an interviewer, you may want to be a little suspicious of a candidate who displays every good attribute. No candidate should be hired primarily for her interview skills, that is, for a one-shot performance.

Indeed, the proliferation of good advice to applicants should probably cause the interviewer to focus even more intently on the candidate's track record. Perhaps someone you find personally uncongenial can demonstrate he'll do the job better than anyone else. This suggests some questions the interviewer must ask himself before the interview:

- What combination of people skills and technical knowledge does it take to do this job?

- How closely will I have to work with this person? Do I have the time to train him?

- Does the position involve representing the organization, either internally or externally?

- How long do I want this person to keep this job? What are her expectations, and can I hold out the prospect that she'll move up?

- What would be the consequences if this person fails or becomes too demanding?

- With whom will this person be working, and how should I involve them in the hiring process?

Finally, the interviewer should have thought through the job offer sufficiently to know how far it can be stretched in terms of compensation and responsibilities. Sometimes, in the interview process, a manager discovers a candidate with skills he didn't even know he needed. How flexible is the hiring situation?

Conducting the Interview

At the outset, you should indicate that this is to be a discussion between equals. While there are exceptions to this rule, if the candidate is highly qualified for the job, you need her as much as she needs you. Keep in mind the factors that can shape this unspoken message: position in the room, body language, the form and tone of your greeting. Even sitting at the same level and in the same kind of chair can signal a mutuality that will put applicants at ease and help you get to know them faster.

Understand how job candidates argue their case. Broadly, these arguments fit into three categories: (1) Identity: "My background fits me perfectly for this job"; (2) Analogy: "My previous experience and skills are transferable"; (3) Interest: "While on paper I might not seem qualified, this is what I've always wanted to do." Any of these arguments may be valid, and we could add a fourth: "I've succeeded at everything I've tried." But identifying the approach the applicant is taking can help you conduct an interview that tells you much more of what you need to know.

Keep in mind that practiced interviewees will do and say whatever they think it takes to get the job offer. Once hired, the savvy ones will know they have leverage, and often try to redefine the job to fit their interests, or blame any failures on a lack of training and support.

Be careful not to feed unrealistic expectations. No matter what you say about a job in an interview, people almost always hear what they want to hear. They'll remember the parts of the job description that play to their strengths, and discount how their areas of weakness could get in the way. Once in the job, and with the best will in the world, they may be resistant to any suggestion that they, rather than the system or the boss, are responsible for any failures in performance.

The interviewer should maintain control of the interview's structure. This means, in general, starting with pleasantries and establishing some rapport, clarifying expectations surrounding the job, moving to the expected questions, then jolting the candidate off his script, and finally leaving him with a clear idea of where he stands. The candidate, for his part, will often have a roughly similar structure in mind—starting with small talk, moving to the fit between job and applicant, and at the end gaining some closure. Let's take the discussion on his terms:

SMALL TALK: Unless something extreme is going on, mention of the weather is usually a loser on either side. A smart applicant will usually find more relevant common ground, expressing, for example, an informed interest in the interviewer's work or a shared area of expertise. Pay attention to the thread of the candidate's small talk: Is she demonstrating empathetic interest in the field or offering covert complaints and excuses? Your talking about the applicant's interests can suggest to her that this organization will be an engaging and comfortable place to work.

FIT: Here, the interviewer has the responsibility to clarify any questions about the nature of the position, then give the candidate a chance to make a pitch. Letting the candidate take the lead for a while can provide lots of insight into him: Does he understand the job? Is he genuinely enthusiastic about it or merely following a script? Does he have a realistic understanding of his potential position in the organization's structure, or is he over-reaching? Is he willing to learn?

Attentive listening can also suggest other questions for the interviewer, including some that may throw the applicant off his script: In this position, you'd have less autonomy than in your last job; how would you manage that? Will the salary and time con-straints of this position meet your needs? You certainly have many of the skills we're looking for, but how do you plan to get up-to-speed in what is, after all, a very different field? How will you feel about reporting to, or managing, someone who holds the same position you did in another company? What special qualities— resources or potential clients—do you bring to us that would set you apart from other applicants?

GAINING CLOSURE: At this point, the candidate will expect to learn where she stands. She will expect the interviewer to ask what other questions she has about the job; often these will include benefits, flex-time opportunities, and the chances for advancement. Once the interviewer has signalled closure, he should pay careful attention to whether the applicant understands and finishes the interview gracefully. This will often suggest volumes about a future employee's capacity to manage time and respond to social signals.

Through it all, be candid about the opportunities and constraints of the position. This includes letting the candidate know how she will be evaluated. Pay careful attention to whether she seems to get these messages.

A good interviewer must also know what not to ask. The list of proscribed questions isn't up to you alone; there are laws, federal and state, about what's off limits. If you're not familiar with the rules in your jurisdiction, make sure you check beforehand with someone in human resources. In general, the guiding principle is to steer clear of controversial or personal topics, unless the applicant brings them up. It's not your business to inquire about his politics, religion, ethnicity, or sexual orientation. Of particular legal sensitivity are questions about the candidate's medical condition, possible status as handicapped, previous legal or grievance procedures against employers, whistle blowing, insurance needs, or criminal record.

> Don't be too quick to dismiss a candidate who seems "overqualified."

Sometimes, especially if you don't sense a "fit," you may choose to describe your organization's culture. "We're a pretty hierarchical organization" or "Anyone here can walk into the President's office at any time." Occasionally the candidate will bring up personal circumstances to make sure the job can accommodate them ("My mother is ill, and I may need to take some unexpected time off"). Thank her for being candid, and tell her whether the job can accommodate such circumstances.

Also avoid questions that are so general that the applicant will have to struggle. "Tell me about yourself" is unlikely to lead anywhere productive. Instead, pick out features of the candidate's résumé and ask him to explain how they fit with the job. Or if you notice a long period of unemployment, you might ask, "What have you been doing since your last job?" The answers may range from homemaking to working on personal projects, and these can lead to interesting lines of inquiry. Don't presume that because a candidate hasn't pursued a relentlessly linear career path that she's inappropriate for a high-pressure job. And don't press too hard on why the person is job-hunting. While it's fine to ask candidates why they are seeking a new position, it's usually inappropriate to ask them what other jobs they may be pursuing.

In all this, be guided by the principle that you're trying to have a conversation, not engage in a verbal duel.

Evaluating the Interview

Often, the candidate that pops to the top in person is not best for the job. This can occur for several natural and human reasons: You may just like the person, be dazzled by their qualifications, or even be moved by compassion for their personal situation. Any of these factors can play a legitimate role in a decision to hire. But before making an offer, take some time for the impact of personality to wear off and to match the leading candidate against your initial checklist once more.

Try to determine whether the person will be happy in the job. Increasingly in today's market, candidates are discounted because they're "overqualified." But if you believe the applicant understands the situation, this may not be a barrier to hiring; in fact, you could be losing a very valuable contributor. A good manager should not be intimidated at the thought of taking on a highly qualified subordinate unless his track record demonstrates an unwillingness to be managed. Conversely, an apparently underqualified candidate may rise to the challenge if she has enough enthusiasm and ambition.

In weighing an insider versus a candidate from outside, bear in mind that an insider is more likely to hit the ground running; she knows the territory. An outsider is likely to bring new skills and a fresh perspective into the organization. Given the position, which combination of these qualities matters more?

And, of course, talk with others in your organization who have interviewed the candidate. Let them help you overcome any biases that may arise from your personal chemistry with the interviewees. At some level, finally, you will have to go with your gut, but, by going through a careful interview process, you can make your abdominal inclination as informed as possible.

For Further Reading

Best Answers to the 201 Most Frequently Asked Interview Questions by Matthew J. DeLuca (1997, McGraw-Hill)

Interviewing by Arlene S. Hirsch (1996, Wiley)

Power Interviews by Neil Yeager and Lee Hough (1990, Wiley)

Reprint U9703C

Use Case Interviewing to Improve Your Hiring

• • •

Melissa Raffoni

What's the biggest constraint on growing your business? When I ask executives this question, nine times out of ten the answer is "Finding quality employees." It's a real problem, especially in these days of 4% unemployment. You want to get people working ASAP—but you also want them to be the right people. You have to balance the need for speedy decisions with the need for thoroughness in your decision making. One useful and often overlooked tool for improving your hiring process is the technique known as case interviewing.

Interviewers using this technique describe a scenario illustrating a business problem the candidate might encounter on the job. Then, during the interview, the candidate is expected to ask a series of questions and ultimately present a solution to the problem. If you're the interviewer, for example, you might describe an industry and ask the candidate what strategy he or she would use to develop a new business in this market.

Case interviewing has been used by strategy consulting firms for years. As former McKinsey or Gemini consultants have moved out into industry, they have taken the technique with them. Frito-Lay, Johnson & Johnson, Kraft, Microsoft, and Dell are among the many companies using it, and it's now spreading to more traditional industries such as retail. Says Jennifer Joyce, project manager in the strategic planning department at Staples: "Case interviewing enables us to see first-hand how a candidate tackles a strategic question and communicates possible solutions. . . . It also pinpoints those who can see the big picture."

Traditionally, case interviewing has focused on testing problem-solving abilities. Interviewers assess candidates' framework for approaching the problem, their logic, and their choice of questions. "The cases I use typically involve either product launches or turning around a declining business," says Stephen H. George, product director at McNeil Consumer Healthcare, a division of Johnson & Johnson. "For example, your management has asked you to launch a new shampoo into the marketplace—take me through your decision steps for creating a launch strategy."

But interviewers can also test skills other than problem solving. An interviewer at McNeil, for instance, could test quantitative acumen by asking candidates how they would approach pricing and forecasting. Sales candidates can be asked how they would position a product to a potential customer. One of my favorite cases involves telling technical professionals that their job is gathering requirements for a new information system from an uncooperative business unit, then asking them how they would approach it.

The power of case interviewing is that it can accomplish several tasks at once:

IT GETS AS CLOSE TO REAL-LIFE SITUATIONS AS POSSIBLE. It's a chance to see someone's mind work with little or no preparation. This allows you to evaluate interviewees who have well-polished answers to conventional questions such as "Where do you want to be in five years?"

IT HELPS CANDIDATES GAIN A BETTER UNDERSTANDING OF THE JOB. I have had many candidates end a case and say, "I was a little unclear about the job before the interview; this gave me a better sense of what's involved."

IT TESTS A VARIETY OF SKILLS. Case interviewing can test competencies such as strategic thinking, analytical ability, and judgment, along with a variety of communication skills, including active listening, questioning, and dealing with confrontation. Particularly for positions where there is no "right" background or "typical" candidate—that is, no requirement for specific degrees or experience—case interviewing allows you to put everyone on the same footing.

Using the case interviewing technique does have its risks and downsides. It can take a lot of time. It can catch candidates so off-guard that they become uncharacteristically uncomfortable or nervous. Case interviewers should monitor the time, clearly communicate the objectives of the case, and make it plain that there is no right answer. Since the technique can't test all competencies, it should not be used alone. For example, to test areas such as teamwork, motivation, or leadership, interviewers should consider innovative alternatives such as group exercises. The most important thing is to define what you want to test and design a format that works for your organization. Case interviewing can be a valuable addition to a well-thought-out hiring process that is continually assessed and improved.

Reprint U9907E

Interviewing Your Prospective Supervisor

with Rich Wellins

• • •

There is nothing more important than an employee's relationship with her boss. Numerous studies have shown that it is the linchpin of great performance, long-term commitment, and employee satisfaction at all levels of the organization. But although most hiring managers will look at the personality fit between themselves and job candidates, few prospective employees give this component very much consideration—often to their regret if they discover later on that they and their supervisors are mismatched.

There are ways for job candidates to hedge against this fate, says Rich Wellins, who, as Senior Vice President at human resources firm Development Dimensions International (DDI), focuses on helping companies put the right people in the right seats. His advice about how to initiate frank discussions with prospective supervisors—and how to get telltale glimpses into their personality—is as relevant to considering a new internal assignment as it is to interviewing for a position in a different company.

Why is it important for job candidates to interview their potential boss?

The primary reason people leave jobs is because of their relationship with their supervisor. It's not because of pay, benefits, or even because of the organizational department; rather, it's because they are not getting along with their supervisor.

Interviewing the prospective supervisor gives the candidate a better opportunity to determine whether this is the sort of person that he can respect and develop a good rapport with. If he feels there's a good fit with the supervisor, then, if he's hired, he's going to be a happier, more engaged employee.

Won't a manager who needs to fill the position tend to be less than candid?

You're not going to eliminate that completely, but a way to get around it is to ask for specifics. Four or five key questions should give you a good handle on the supervisor's style.

Questions such as, "What sort of working style do you have?" or "Do you believe empowerment is important?" or "Do you have opportunities for growth and development?" won't do the trick. Instead, ask for specific examples: "How have you successfully mentored someone on your team? How have you helped someone achieve her professional goals? Can you give me examples of techniques you used to get your team to collaborate better?"

Any particulars you should look for?

Pretty much everybody wants opportunities for growth. And no one wants to be micromanaged. Also, does the supervisor have good listening skills? And do the types of questions he asks indicate that he's genuinely interested in you and in having the best possible working relationship with you?

Beyond these things, there aren't any universal attributes to look for. It's more a matter of determining the optimal conditions for you as an individual. For some employees, it's essential to have a boss who'll give them a lot of coaching. For others, that may not be as important as having a great deal of independence.

Can you make reliable inferences based on the way a supervisor interacts with her team?

It's doubtful that you'll get much of a chance to do that,

beyond perhaps seeing how she interacts with other employees. But even that can be significant—the way she treats those people tells you something about her social intelligence.

It is totally appropriate, however, especially if you're in the buyer's seat, to ask if you can interview a few people who work for the supervisor. Doing that can give you a much fuller picture of the job's challenges and opportunities.

Are there more indirect ways of discovering what the supervisor is really like?

What do the potential supervisor's tone and manner tell you? Does he answer your questions? Pay attention to his nonverbal communication, too. For example, does he maintain eye contact? What does he have on his desk? All these things can tell you a little bit about his values, personality, and management style. In addition, look at how you've been treated throughout the interview process. You'll find clues here about not only your potential boss but also the organizational culture.

Reprint U0410B

Don't Ask These Questions!

How to Avoid Breaking the Law in a Job Interview

• • •

Heather C. Liston

"I'm not really allowed to ask you this," the company president began, "but I want to know if you're married or planning to get married soon, because I lose women that way." I was 28 years old, happily single, and dedicated to building my career—so I answered the question he wasn't supposed to ask. No, I said; I had no plans to make any changes in my personal life. I was ready to commit myself to his company, and no pesky family obligations were going to interfere. I got the job, but I've often regretted my answer. By cooperating with the president, I had unintentionally thwarted a law I believe in—a law designed to give all of us a fair chance to earn a living in a world full of prejudices.

Even if you trust yourself to be fair, you have a legal responsibility, as an employer, to know what are and are not appropriate questions to ask of candidates applying for positions at your company. The Equal Employment Opportunity Commission (EEOC), established under Title VII of the Civil Rights Act of 1964, has the mandate to protect us from improper discrimination in employment. The relevant laws enforced by the EEOC are:

- Title VII of the Civil Rights Act of 1964, which prohibits employment discrimination on the basis of race, color, religion, sex, and national origin.

- The Age Discrimination in Employment Act of 1967 (ADEA), which prohibits discrimination on the basis of age for people who are 40 or older.

- Titles I and V of the Americans with Disabilities Act of 1990 (ADA), which prohibits discrimination on the basis of mental and physical disability.

(The text of each of these laws is available through the EEOC's Web site at www.eeoc.gov, or by calling 800-669-4000.)

Don't Ask About Protected Categories

How does this affect you as an employer and interviewer? "Federal Civil Rights law does not specifically bar you from asking anything except age [over 40]," says Thomas H. Nail, who is president of Thomas Houston Associates, Inc., a human resources consulting firm, and a member of the National Workplace Diversity Committee of the Society for Human Resources Management.

> You have a legal responsibility, as an employer, to know what are and are not appropriate questions to ask of candidates.

"The problem is that the information you obtain if you ask certain questions can get you in a whole lot of trouble. That's why the human resources profession is working to help people steer clear of potential problems by avoiding certain kinds of questions." These questions, naturally, are equally dangerous whether they come up on written applications or in oral job interviews.

The Massachusetts Commission Against Discrimination (MCAD) provides a clear statement of the general rule, which can serve as a guideline for applying federal law as well: "An employer should generally not ask on a job application or during an interview any question that:

- identifies a person as being within a protected category;

- results in the screening out of members in a protected category; or

- is not a valid basis for predicting successful job performance."

The New York State Human Rights law states an important exception to general prohibitions against discrimination, the "Bona Fide Occupational Qualification" exception: "It is permissible to make pre-employment inquiries relating to the applicant's age, race, creed, color, national origin, sex, marital status or disability, where such inquiries are based upon a bona fide occupational qualification."

The Nine Worst Questions

That's a sampling of the legal terrain. Now let's get specific. Here are some examples of things not to ask:

1. *"How old are you?"* or *"What year were you born?"*

You may ask whether the applicant is over 18. Technically, federal law provides protection against age discrimination only for those over 40, but it's safer not to start asking questions like "Are you over 39?" You should also avoid language that is designed to elicit information about age, such as "When did you graduate from college?"

2. *"Are you married?"* (or engaged, or involved, or divorced) or *"Do you prefer to be called Mrs., Miss, or Ms.?"*

Forget it. You may ask whether the candidate has responsibilities that will interfere with specific job requirements, such as travel. But if you're asking women this, you better make sure you're asking your male candidates as well. Marital status, according to Robert Sanders, director of the Boston-area office of the EEOC, is not itself a federally protected category. But if it can be shown that you're treating men and women differently by asking members of only one gender about their marital status, this is covered as a "sex-plus" violation, meaning it becomes gender discrimination. (And again, certain states do provide specific protection for marital status.)

3. *"Do you attend church services?"* or *"What religious holidays do you observe?"*

You may not inquire about religious denominations or affiliations, unless you happen to be hiring for a position at a religious organization. Karen Walsh, employment and employee relations manager for the First Church of Christ, Scientist, in Boston, says, "Religion, in this organization, is considered a bona fide job qualification. Our function is to promote our religion, and it

Check State and Local Laws Too

Be sure you know the relevant regional differences where you do business. Most states and some local governments have antidiscrimination laws of their own, which often provide protection beyond what the federal government requires. For example, the Massachusetts Commission Against Discrimination adds "sexual orientation" to the list of protected categories within the commonwealth. Virginia and New York add "marital status" and "age" to their lists of protected categories. Federal law protects only those over 40 from age discrimination, but your state may require that you probe no further than to ascertain whether a candidate is over 18. New York State does not offer special protection against discrimination based on sexual orientation, but New York City does. And some states provide specific protection for people with sickle cell traits (which can be related to race).

would be difficult for those who don't understand the religion or adhere to its tenets to do the job of communicating to the public about it. If I can't find a Christian Scientist, though, I open the doors and I can no longer discriminate. Working for a religious organization does not give me the right, for example, to say I'd prefer a Methodist to a Jew."

4. *"What is your native language?"*

If the position requires fluency in a particular language you may, of course, ask whether the applicant speaks that language. Otherwise, steer clear, since this question could elicit information about national origin.

5. *"Where did your parents come from?"*

You may ask whether the applicant is legally eligible to work in the United States, but avoid any other questions with implications about citizenship or national origin.

6. *"What is your maiden name?"*

None of your business. You may, however, ask whether the applicant has ever worked for your company before under a different name.

7. *"What is your complexion or skin color?"*

Be serious. Race and color are not bona fide qualifications for any job.

8. *"Have you ever been arrested?"*

Don't go there. It is acceptable, however, to ask if the applicant has been convicted of a crime. Although questions about arrest do not immediately appear to be related to the Civil Rights law, there is a logic to this, according to Nail. "If you look at a sampling of who gets arrested in the U.S.," he explains, "without factoring in convictions, you'll find that more minorities are arrested. So making arrest records a factor in your hiring process is neutral on its face but has the effect of discriminating against minorities." And keep in mind that certain states make explicit prohibitions against questions relating to arrest and/or conviction records.

9. *"Do you have any disabilities?"*

"Since 1964, you'd have to be living under a rock not to know about the basic civil rights requirements," says Sanders. "So most of the questions and cases we get at the EEOC now are about the Americans with Disabilities Act, which is the new kid on the block that we enforce." The document to get to help you understand this law is the "ADA Enforcement Guidance: Pre-Employment Disability-Related Questions and Medical Examinations" issued in 1995, which is available from the EEOC. The law prohibits both direct inquiries on forbidden subjects (like "Are you handicapped?") and indirect inquiries that are "likely to elicit information about a disability" (like "Have you ever received workers' compensation?").

You may ask whether an applicant is able to perform specific job functions. You can even ask him or her to demonstrate their ability to do so, as long as you're asking all candidates applying for the same job category to give the same demonstration. And—don't worry—you do have the right to find out about any relevant medical problems before a final job offer is made. The goal of this law is just to "isolate an employer's consideration of an applicant's nonmedical qualifications from any con-

> ## Race and color are not bona fide qualifications for any job.

sideration of the applicant's medical condition." Therefore, the ADA states that "an employer may ask disability-related questions and require medical examinations of an applicant only after the applicant has been given a conditional job offer."

"There is usually going to be a subjective element in hiring," says Walsh. "But the laws are good because they remind us all to think about what we're doing. If it's your natural tendency to feel like hiring people who look like you, for example, you now have to stop and say, 'Wait a minute—is there any reason a person in a wheelchair couldn't do this job?'"

One of the challenging things about job interviewing is that it's not an entirely controlled, automatic transaction. It's basically a conversation between two people, who are trying to decide whether they'll be happy bumping

Where to Look and Whom to Call for Further Information

Dorca Gomez, commissioner of the MCAD, says, "It's hard to keep it all in your head at once, what you're allowed to ask and what you're not, and it can get fairly complex. But we offer a Pre-Employment Inquiries Fact Sheet to help employers. And they can always call us if they have a question. It's better to be sure. Some employers seem to be afraid of us, but they're our clients too; this shouldn't be adversarial."

New York State's Division of Human Rights also makes available a helpful document, "Pre-Employment Rulings on Inquiries." You can read it on their Web site at www.nysdhr.com or call 212-961-8400 to have it sent to you. And the relevant restrictions contained in the Civil Rights Act of 1964 are best explained in the EEOC's "Pre-Employment Inquiry Guidelines" of 1981, which can be ordered by calling 800-669-EEOC.

For those who want to learn more, the EEOC holds regular Technical Assistance and Training Programs. More information about them is available at their Web site (www.eeoc.gov) or at 800-669-4000. The Society for Human Resource Management, which is located in Alexandria, Virginia, can be reached at 703-548-3440 or www.shrm.org.

into each other at the photocopier five days a week for the next few years. The human implications of acquiring new coworkers make it only natural that we want to bring some humanity to our first meetings with them too. "Most people prefer an informal interview," says Dan Relton, vice president of human resources for New York City-based Grey Communications, Inc. "So these things often come up—people will mention whether they have children or whom they live with—and that's fine. But I only ask things that are relevant to the job."

For Further Reading

Fair, Square, and Legal: Safe Hiring, Managing & Firing Practices to Keep You and Your Company Out of Court by Donald H. Weiss (1995, AMACOM)

Hiring the Best: A Manager's Guide to Effective Interviewing by Martin Yate (1993, Adams Media Corp.)

Reprint C9906B

Assess Candidates' Cultural Fit

• • •

The right technical skills and industry knowledge are no longer enough to define the "perfect" hire. In addition to skills and knowledge, new employees must fit with your unit's or company's culture. That means they need to demonstrate the values your company emphasizes, as well as the attitudes and behaviors (such as friendliness to customers, openness to new ideas, and emotional intelligence) needed to support your company's competitive strategy.

The articles in this section provide practices for assessing job candidates' potential cultural fit—including using personality tests and asking behavior-related questions during interviews. But ensuring a good cultural fit also requires you, the manager, to be willing to hire people who differ markedly from you in temperament and abilities—so that each member of your team brings complementary personalities to the job. For example, to assemble a top-notch team, you may need to select newcomers who possess a strong entrepreneurial bent. And as you'll see, you will also have to develop strategies for handling the inevitable friction that arises when people with contrasting temperaments collaborate.

Cultural Fit

Why Hiring Good People
Is No Longer Good Enough

• • •

David Stauffer

"*Oi vey,* if it's not one thing, then it's another thing," rue today's human-resource managers. No sooner do they finish playing designated executioners in the corporate downsizings of recent years than they are confronted with a tight market for skilled labor, the likes of which hasn't been seen in decades. Good people and good searches cost more than ever. And the criteria for determining who's right for the job are now both more extensive and harder to assess.

Simply put, hiring mistakes are more immediately

obvious—and more expensive to fix. Which is why respected CEOs and executive search consultants alike are now placing much more emphasis on interpersonal skills and the fit between the candidate and the organization's culture.

Don't Settle for the "Near Fit"

"Greatness starts with superb people," write leadership gurus Warren Bennis and Patricia Ward Biederman. Their book *Organizing Genius: The Secrets of Creative Collaboration* examines seven remarkable collaborations—including the Manhattan Project, which built the first atomic bomb, and the Walt Disney Studio—"in the hope of finding out how their collective magic is made." This analysis leads to 15 "take-home lessons," the ingredients of excellence that are essential for developing "Great Groups."

"Recruiting the most talented people possible is the first task," Bennis and Biederman maintain. "They are the ones who spot the gaps in what we know. They discover and solve problems." These people are the best of the best because "leaders of Great Groups love talent" and "are confident enough to recruit people better than themselves. . . . In Great Groups the right person has the right job. Truly gifted people are never interchangeable."

If the concept of the Great Group were enlarged to include a modern corporation, chances are the best candidate would be General Electric. GE's phenomenal growth over the 20-year tenure of chairman Jack Welch owed much to Welch's determination to hire only the best. At a 1997 meeting with his top executives, for example, Welch is reported to have insisted that any "C-level performers" be shown a pink slip and the nearest exit. GE, he said, is an A+ company.

In the spate of books about Bill Gates and the corporate juggernaut he built, none fails to mention the role of recruiting in the company's rise to preeminence. In *The Microsoft Way: The Real Story of How the Company Outsmarts Its Competition,* for example, author Randall E. Stross claims that Microsoft "has pursued the best more successfully than other companies, and has visibly reaped the rewards more dramatically than others, too." A key component of the Microsoft recruiting strategy is preferring an open slot to a "near fit." Stross quotes Gates from a company video on hiring: "If you have somebody who's mediocre...we're really in big trouble," because the less-than-ideal employee is hard to dismiss. "Thus," Stross concludes, "Gates admonished his recruiters not to settle for second best or a near fit, even if a continuing vacancy creates hardship."

Insist on a "Values Match"

As the collaborations described in *Organizing Genius* demonstrate, there's nothing new in requiring an exact fit between job candidate and job opening. But the very fact that this standard is so often characterized as exceptional indicates that it is still not widely practiced. Evidence from various quarters, however, suggests that the definition of "perfect fit" is being expanded beyond the range of attributes that can be listed on a résumé. Increasingly, organizations are also focusing on what an executive recruiter calls the "soft characteristics": how likely candidates are to fit into the corporate culture.

Precisely what are these soft skills? GE's Welch enumerated several of them when he said, according to the *Washington Post*, "We would not knowingly hire anyone in our company that wasn't 'boundaryless,' that wasn't open to an idea from anywhere, that wasn't excited about a learning environment." Welch, the *Post* article went on, "said GE is quite willing to toss out managers who don't sign on to the culture, even if they produce good results. 'We take people with great results and ask them to move on to other companies because they don't have our values.'" It is this insistence on a "values match"—over and above a talents-and-responsibilities match—that is gaining approbation and prominence.

Among those leading the charge is Stanford Business School professor Jerry I. Porras, coauthor of *Built to Last: Successful Habits of Visionary Companies,* a 1994 book that profiled 18 exemplary U.S. firms. Selection figures prominently in Porras's efforts to help organizations formulate visions that lead to superior performance. Creating "alignment" is essential, he says. It results from determining "the five or six key behaviors we need in our people to realize our envisioned future. For example, everyone in the Disney organization must strive always to be pleasant to customers for customers to have the magical experience the company envisions."

This may be a trickier task than it seems, Porras notes, "because you don't sell the vision—someone either holds the core value or doesn't. The most that the leadership team can do is help people understand the vision." As for those who don't hold the core value, Porras contends that "you'll eventually have to part company, because, over the long haul, it's not good for the individual or the company to maintain the association. And in some cases this will be a very tough bullet to bite, because the person might in some ways—for example, technical ex-pertise—be a valuable contributor to the organization."

Millington F. McCoy, managing director of executive search consultants Gould, McCoy & Chadick, would probably agree with Porras's hard advice—soft skills have simply become that critical. Continual rapid change in organizations has altered the mix of critical skills that top managers need, she explains. "Because organizations are less hierarchical, newly matrixed, and more global, executives must be able to work effectively in teams that bring together diverse people, skills, and talents. That requires greater strength in what I call the soft character-istics—not just a great résumé, but a cultural fit with my client organization."

The need to look beyond the traditional bounds of

strengths that can be stated on a résumé is indicated by the changing value of intellectual brilliance in and of itself. Increasingly, McCoy says, brilliance has a questionable net benefit to organizations when it is unaccompanied by strong interpersonal skills. "Sometimes an organization becomes enamored of pure brilliance and hires a candidate on that strength alone. But the brilliant person who lacks basic interpersonal skills can quickly become isolated—and therefore ineffective."

Similarly, the new ideal skills set de-emphasizes ego. "You often find high insecurity behind a high ego," McCoy declares. "And insecurity may often be expressed by a leader as attempts to control every work situation. In today's matrix workplace, that just won't work." So what qualities have moved to the forefront? "High levels of emotional maturity and interpersonal skills that are stronger today than ever before," she responds.

Tips on Searching

Advice for anyone with a hand in hiring decisions: assess candidates' "cultural fit" *before* you make them employees. *The Microsoft Way* author Stross lists several means by which Microsoft does this:

Look All the Time

Microsoft recruiters assume that the most desirable candidates aren't looking because they don't have to look—they attract unsolicited offers. This mindset implies a recruiting effort unconstrained by budget or staffing levels. In *Hard Drive: Bill Gates and the Making of the Microsoft Empire,* authors James Wallace and Jim Erickson quote a top Microsoft executive: "Do we have a head-count budget? No way. There are some guys you meet only once in a lifetime."

Favor Potential Over Experience

Stross says Gates and his recruiters "aren't overly concerned about relevant experience," but are instead biased "toward intelligence or smartness over anything else, even, in many cases, experience."

Seek a Specific Sort of Intelligence

Brains alone are insufficient to make it as a Microsoftie, Stross claims. Those who are exactly right are "pragmatically inclined, verbally agile, and able to respond deftly when challenged." That makes for a harrowing job interview. *Hard Drive* describes grillings of candidates that included tough math and logic problems and "difficult questions that had nothing to do with programming." A recruiter explains, "We wanted to know if they were driven enough, so we could drop them into our atmosphere and have them thrive."

Rest in Peace, *Kemo Sabe*

"Collaboration is a necessity," write Bennis and Biederman, for a group to be great: certain tasks "can only be performed collaboratively. [So] Great Groups are full of talented people who can work together. Sharing information and advancing the work are the only real social obligations. . . . The Lone Ranger, the incarnation of the individual problem solver, is dead."

If by now you're thinking that all these broader and more stringent search criteria make it tougher than ever to find the perfect person for that key slot—you're right. "One pronounced effect on our searches today," McCoy points out, "is that many of them are now automatically global in scope." Yes, she acknowledges, that makes the job much more challenging for her and other search consultants. "But a world of ongoing, dramatic change is also much more challenging for our client organizations and for the candidate executives, isn't it?"

For Further Reading

Built to Last: Successful Habits of Visionary Companies by Jerry I. Porras and James C. Collins (1994, HarperBusiness)

Hard Drive: Bill Gates and the Making of the Microsoft Empire by James Wallace and Jim Erickson (1992, HarperBusiness)

The Microsoft Way: The Real Story of How the Company Outsmarts Its Competition by Randall E. Stross (1996, Addison-Wesley)

Organizing Genius: The Secrets of Creative Collaboration by Warren Bennis and Patricia Ward Biederman (1997, Addison-Wesley)

Reprint U9803C

Personality Tests in Hiring

How to Do It Right

• • •

Edward Prewitt

The use of psychological testing to screen job applicants is growing. In a June 1998 American Management Association survey, 45% of 1,085 member companies reported administering one or more tests to job applicants, up from 35% in 1997 (the first year AMA tracked test usage). Because of the time and expense involved, these tests are more often given to prospective managers than to lower-level employees, for whom tests of job skills are often more appropriate.

Should you and your company be using psychological testing? On the one hand, experts counsel caution. Unlike college-entrance exams, pre-employment tests aren't a rubber ruler for arbitrarily weeding out candidates. They can't provide a magic solution to your company's turnover problems. What's more, if you use the wrong test—or ask even a single inappropriate question—you expose your company to the threat of a lawsuit.

"I know an attorney who does employment law who's very happy when companies use tests for selection—because that's how she makes her living," says James Waldroop, a business psychologist who is also associate director of the MBA Career Development Program at Harvard Business School. "We all want backup for our decisions, but tests are just too risky."

So why give these tests at all? One big reason: used properly, psychological tests may predict success on the job better than any other measure. Powell & Wagner Associates, a psychology consulting firm, conducted three follow-up studies of executives it had screened for corporate clients. The studies all found a high correlation between the firm's ratings of prospective managers who were later hired and the rate of subsequent termination (both voluntary and involuntary) of those managers. Moreeover, a statistical comparison showed that the company's screening process—psychological testing followed by interviews—outperformed all other methods of assessing candidates, including interviews, references, career history, and even six-month performance reviews.

Studies by the people who do the testing, of course, may not be definitive. But testing has some built-in advantages, such as a lack of bias, over other means of selection. A test asks the same questions and applies the same standards to everyone, and can thus counterbalance an interviewer's stereotypes. "In one firm we worked with, the CEO had a fit over two things: if [applicants] were heavy, and if they didn't go to the right school," says James McSherry, a senior partner of the psychology consulting firm McSherry, Diedrich & Stevens. "Those aren't exactly the best predictors of success. But everyone has biases. What a good [pre-employment] test does is use questions that are valid and accurate."

Psychological tests can also give a sense of how a prospective employee would fare within a company's culture. "It happens so often that a person goes through all the interviews, gets hired, comes into a company, and then in a short time finds it's not a good fit," says Douglas Powell of Powell & Wagner. "There's lots of turnover in companies still, because company culture and [a new employee's] expectations are very different."

Maybe your organization is already using tests in hiring—or maybe you're considering doing so. If so, here are tips from experts on how to make testing work for you.

Specify Your Hiring Needs

American Golf Corporation has 1,000 managers overseeing more than 14,000 other employees in 270 locations across the country. American Golf has for years required all prospective managers to fill out a commercially available personality measure called the Predictive Index. "It has been useful," says Tom Norton, director of recruiting. "What we're careful of is matching [applicants'] personality or work style to the supervisor they'd be working for. If someone really likes working with people and requires a lot of supervision, he or she probably wouldn't work well with an introvert."

American Golf's approach illustrates one of the main requirements (and advantages) of psychological tests: knowing what you're looking for. "It's important to look at what characteristics are being used in the job. That helps to guide what tests should be used," says William Harris, executive director of the Association of Test Publishers, a trade association. McSherry says that "getting people to think about what they really need in a new hire" is one of his firm's most important services to clients. Before administering tests, the firm questions clients on the specific requirements of the job in question and on the values and behavior that define the client's corporate culture. "What we do is work on getting the criteria for optimum behavior really clear."

Indeed, some think that the self-study a company should undergo in preparation for using pre-employment tests is the most valuable component of the process. "If I want to use psychological tests, what do I have to do? I have to get really clear about what I want and then I have to design an interview that gets at that information," Waldroop says. "Well, that's what I should be doing anyway."

Don't Rely on Tests Alone

"We think of [testing] as one of three legs on a stool, where the other two are interviews and the candidate's track record," says Powell. "There is no single watershed criterion for hiring someone." Powell's clients prescreen their candidates through interviews, but then trained interviewers on Powell's staff conduct intensive follow-up interviews. At American Golf, the personality measure "is one piece of many, many things we look at for each candidate," according to Norton. "It can validate other opinions we gather from things like interviews and references. It can sometimes raise an issue to look further into. [The test] is never anything we base a hiring decision on by itself."

More Is Better (Up to a Point)

Tests aren't one-size-fits-all. To test for personality traits, experts advise instruments such as the Personality Research Form, WAIS-R, or the Executive Profile Survey; to examine a candidate's interests, the Jackson Vocational Interest Survey; and to measure cognitive ability (the term that has replaced IQ), a test like the Watson-Glaser Critical Thinking Appraisal. It's not uncommon for companies and their consultants to give candidates several different tests at one sitting—one each for personality, interests, integrity, and cognitive ability, for example. "People ask why we don't use just one test. Extra tests bring out that extra 10% of information," Powell says. Adds Harris of the Association of Test Publishers: "As you start moving toward a battery of tests in which each has some variance, you increase predictive power." To be sure, testers (like any professionals) like to sell more of their services rather than fewer, and the cost of testing will rise as more tests are administered. But where senior executives are concerned, the extra money may be small compared to the cost of a bad hire.

Hire a Consultant

Psychological testing is not for amateurs. Proper interpretation of results, even results of an off-the-shelf test, takes doctoral-level training in statistics, testing, and assessment. The services of a consulting psychologist typically run about $1,500 to $2,000 per candidate, Powell and McSherry say. The more extensive a screening, the higher the cost; Powell may charge $2,500 for a top executive.

To prevent misuse, distribution of the most powerful tests is strictly controlled. Tests such as the Jackson Personality Inventory, the 16PF Personality Profile, and the Guilford-Zimmerman Temperament Survey, are available only to members of organizations such as the American Psychological Association. Although there are no licensing requirements for test-givers and test consultants, the APA serves as a de facto licensing board, and psychologists found to have applied tests improperly can be decertified. "Everybody is very, very careful today," McSherry says. "You don't use these tests lightly. [Clients] test us and test our track record before they'll use us."

Beware of Pitfalls

One factor forcing testers themselves to be very, very careful is the threat of lawsuits. Several laws and regulations of recent years—the Equal Employment Opportunity Commission's rules, Congress's prohibition of lie detectors, and, most significantly, the American Disabilities Act of 1990 (ADA)—sharply restrict the content of pre-employment tests. "We can only use about 10% of the tests we used to use," says Powell, who has administered psychological tests for 32 years. The remainder fall afoul of rules prohibiting invasiveness. Retail chain Target Stores, for instance, goofed by giving job applicants its own test, which included questions from two standard tests that predated the ADA. The test included a few now-taboo questions on health, sexual preference, and religious beliefs. Target was sued in 1991 for employment discrimination and settled out of court for $2 million.

To be legally bulletproof, all questions on a pre-employment test must have "predictive validity," Mc-

Sherry says. That is, the test-giver must be able to show not only that a test accurately measures the traits it seeks to measure, but that it also predicts behavior in the specific job in question. That's no small task, so test developers routinely spend millions of dollars and months or years on large-scale field studies before releasing a test. "The more controls a publisher has to ensure that valid questions are being asked and the more qualified a consultant is, the safer you are," says Harris.

It is feasible for companies to construct their own tests, complete with predictive validity. "Procter & Gamble does this and they do it very well," Waldroop says. "They've done their homework on it. They designed a test that accurately, validly distinguishes the performance of a brand manager." Unless you have a great deal of expertise, money, and time to devote to making in-house tests, however, you should rely on published tests and expert consultants.

For Further Reading

Model Guidelines for Pre-employment Integrity Testing, Second Edition (1996, Association of Test Publishers)

"Job Skill Testing and Psychological Measurement," Research Report supplement (1998, American Management Association)

Reprint U9810C

Hiring (Emotionally) Smart

. . .

When Multi-Health Systems (MHS), tested 1,500 U.S. Air Force recruiters for emotional intelligence, it identified five attributes that separated those who made 100% of their quotas from those who made 70% or below. MHS assigned relative weights to the attributes and they became the basis for a formula for hiring new recruiters. Among the 250–300 people the Air Force hired using this formula, the retention rate shot up by 92%. Factoring in the costs of hiring, training, and settling a new recruit into a position, this translated into a $2.7 million savings.

Nobody questions the importance of emotional intelligence for leadership. Indeed, studies indicate that your emotional intelligence or emotional quotient (EQ) accounts for 15%–45% of your success on the job. (Your IQ, by comparison, is said to account for less than 6%.) Moreover, notes author Daniel Goleman, in a 1996 study of a global food and beverage company, where senior managers had a critical mass of emotional intelligence, their divisions outperformed yearly earnings goals by 20%. Division leaders without that critical mass underperformed by almost the same amount.

In the past, however, it's been difficult to apply the principles of emotional intelligence to everyday situations. But now that's changing. MHS and other companies have developed assessment tools that can be incorporated into hiring, performance-appraisal, and executive-development processes. And results like those achieved by the Air Force are making companies take notice—especially in the current climate, in which competitive strategy depends upon the ability to hire and retain top-notch workers.

"For us, it was a matter of getting a better understanding of all the people we were bringing in," says Shelley Ross, human resources specialist at Wrigley Canada. "As with most companies, our corporate culture has changed over the course of the '90s. We now need people who are more flexible, more committed to satisfying the customer. We've also moved to more of a team-based approach throughout our plants, so we need people with better decision-making skills." Wrigley Canada started using MHS's emotional intelligence test on all prospective hires in 1998. Previously, the company had used a personality assessment for professional and supervisory positions only.

In both examples, the MHS test used is called the EQ-i, developed by psychologist Reuven Bar-On, who says it is the only test registered by the esteemed Buros Institute's *Mental Measurement Yearbook*. A self-report instrument, the EQ-i rates respondents' answers using five composite scales: intrapersonal, interpersonal, adaptability, stress management, and general mood. These five scales are broken down into 15 subscale scores. Each test costs $30–$35 and takes about 40 minutes to complete.

How useful is the EQ-i? Wrigley's results have shown the instrument to be "an accurate tool," Ross concludes. Typically, the test is administered after an initial interview with the hiring manager and a representative from HR. The results can point to aspects of the candidate's social or self-management skills that bear further investigation. "Later in the process," says Ross, "the hiring manager and team members can use the test results to fine-tune their questions of the candidate. I find that the test helps me with reference checking in a similar way."

"A person should never be hired based on test results alone," cautions MHS president and CEO Steven Stein. Prior experience, education, references, interviews, and even sample assignments should all be factored into the decision. But that said, how can you implement the principles of emotional intelligence in your own company's hiring processes? The route MHS took with the Air Force is the most thorough, but if you have constraints, start by administering an emotional intelligence test to all job candidates. Then use tables MHS has developed—they list the most important EQ components for a variety of job classifications—to identify the best applicants.

If an emotional intelligence test seems too involved, says Sandra Yingling, Ph.D., senior consultant at Hay Group, "you can conduct 'behavioral-event interviewing' instead. For example, you ask a candidate to describe a time when she felt frustrated by someone who didn't understand her idea. In the candidate's response, you listen for how she decoded the reactions of the other people around the table at the time of the misunderstanding. At Hay, we've developed a dictionary of emotional competencies that we use to assess the level of emotional sophistication in a candidate's descriptions."

"The whole idea of recruiting is to get someone who fits the job and the culture," says Wrigley's Ross. "We've discovered that it's worth the effort to find someone who's a better match." And EQ is becoming an increasingly important tool for that search.

For Further Reading

The EQ Edge: Emotional Intelligence and Your Success by Steven J. Stein and Howard E. Book (2000, Stone Bridge Press)

Working with Emotional Intelligence by Daniel Goleman (2000, Bantam)

REPRINT U0009C

Managers: To Make a Good Hire, Take a Good Look Inside

●　●　●

Liz Simpson

Management's real genius is turning complexity and specialization into performance," writes Joan Magretta in her book, *What Management Is*. "The more we need to work through others, the better we need to understand ourselves." Yet most hiring processes, whether they emphasize attitudes or skill sets, focus exclusively on the candidates. That's unfortunate, because as Magretta suggests, the greater the hiring manager's self-awareness, the better the new hire is likely to perform.

Effective hiring managers know their strengths and weaknesses as well as where their energies are best spent. They are forthright in describing these things to job candidates and new hires. Like a company forming a strategic alliance with another, such managers select "partners" whose strengths augment the overall ability of the team to meet its objectives. Often, this means the managers will choose candidates with temperaments or ideologies markedly different from their own—but when they do so, they are careful to establish ground rules that enable even polar opposites to work together.

Managers who give in to the "just like me" bias, hiring candidates who are almost carbon copies of themselves, are only setting themselves up for failure. The tendency to feel more comfortable around and give preference to people with a similar education, ethnic/racial background, socioeconomic status, and industry perspective is well documented. It's also potentially lethal in an economy that seems to demand that companies have it all: deep technical skills, broad perspective, and extensive experience, as well as powerful intuition and great people sensitivities.

Using Colleagues as a Mirror

"Accurate self-assessors"—people with a realistic sense of their own strengths and weaknesses—"are better able to improve their performance," write researchers Dianne

Nilsen and David P. Campbell in a 1993 study. But time, experience, and solitary reflection aren't foolproof teachers in the quest to develop the necessary self-awareness. To strip away the layers of self-deception, you often need others' help. "Knowledgeable observers give more valid, accurate ratings" of a manager's human relations skills—including the ability to attract and develop talent—than the manager herself, Nilsen and Campbell continue.

Nora Denzel, senior vice president in Hewlett-Packard's software global business unit, got plenty of opportunities to receive constructive criticism early in her career, when she worked at IBM. There, she says, personality instruments like the Myers-Briggs, videotaped exercises, and regular 360-degree feedback helped her become more aware of her strengths and limitations. As a result, she developed the maturity and self-confidence required to be candid about the kinds of behavior she could and could not tolerate, which has made the hiring and motivating work she does in her current job much easier. "Rather than trying to sell candidates the job, I'm almost convincing them not to work with me unless there's a strong likelihood that our working relationship will be productive for both of us," she says.

Owning up to your shortcomings "is easier to do with technical skills," says Carol Daly, vice president of business development at Ricoh, a leading manufacturer of office automation equipment. "For example, if I didn't know anything about Web browsers, I'd hire someone who did. When it comes to more intangible skills, like communication or networking, it's harder to admit your shortcomings. But it's essential to set your ego aside and realize you're not the only hero on your team." Like Denzel, Daly learned to overcome her discomfort with direct feedback about her blind spots while at IBM, where employees rated their supervisor and their supervisor's boss annually.

"The biggest change for me during my career has been my ability to be honest about my vulnerabilities," says Denzel. "Before, I would try to hide them, but given the amount of hours you spend with your team, there's nothing they don't eventually know about you. If you are in denial, you just don't get such a high-performing team."

A Structured Approach to Preventing Selection Bias

Caterpillar's Engine Center, uses a more formal process to guard against the "just like me" bias. Internal organizational effectiveness consultant Patrick O'Brien gathers objective evaluations of promotion candidates and potential hires based on their skills, qualifications, and talents. Toward the end of the interview process, when it looks like there may be a fit with a candidate, O'Brien brings in an assessment tool that helps the hiring manager understand her own information-processing style and compare it with that of the potential hire, or the whole team, to identify where the alignments or gaps are.

Such two-person or team analyses have helped nearly 200 of Caterpillar's managers mitigate the interpersonal problems that can occur between people whose work strategies are very different.

"It's one thing to hire great talent who can do just what's needed for the job but quite another to ensure the manager values the different things that person brings to their team," says O'Brien. "For some managers, that's tough, and we have to remind them that the success of the project is bigger than they are. Leaders have to understand that people who are very different from them must be engaged differently if they are to succeed."

Ensuring That the Friction Is Creative

If you want your group to be creative, write Dorothy Leonard and Walter Swap in *When Sparks Fly,* you as the leader can't simply tolerate dissent—you must encourage it. Otherwise, your unit will be unable to free itself from "the expectations of how something (or someone) normally functions." It will get "stuck in the mud of approaching a problem from the 'obvious' direction." And it will tend to pay attention only to evidence that confirms the views it already holds.

The challenge, therefore, when you're adding new members, is to bring as much intellectual diversity as you can into your group while ensuring that the resultant friction between varying perspectives and approaches works to improve business results and not to promote interpersonal strife. One way to do this is to define the boss-subordinate relationship right up front. When you're talking to finalists for a position, be explicit about your preferred style of working and the behaviors you do and don't like from subordinates, advise INSEAD researchers Jean-François Manzoni and Jean-Louis Barsoux in their book, *The Set-Up-to-Fail Syndrome*. Such candid communication early on in an employee's tenure

When a New Hire Comes on Board: A Few Caveats

The first few weeks set the tone for the boss-subordinate relationship, but sometimes your best managerial intentions can backfire, say INSEAD researchers Jean-François Manzoni and Jean-Louis Barsoux:

- **Don't expect** the new hire, even one with years of work experience, to be instantly operational.
- **Don't rattle off** a multitude of responsibilities without making clear the two or three dimensions on which the subordinate *must* excel.
- **Don't assume** that any overt criticism will poison the relationship.
- **Don't assume** that the new hire will come to you for advice if he runs into trouble. Often, he won't even realize he needs help.

helps avoid a downward spiral that begins when a supervisor starts to view an employee as suspect.

Worrying that the employee's performance is subpar, the supervisor scrutinizes the employee more closely. The employee begins to feel he's not part of the supervisor's in-group; his confidence falters, his motivation sags, and his performance suffers in response to what he perceives as the supervisor's lowered expectations. The supervisor interprets this withdrawal as confirmation that the employee is indeed a poor performer. The misperceptions and underperformance thus reinforce each other, creating a vicious circle.

But the interview stage can sometimes be too early to spot the friction caused by contrasting attitudes or work styles. That's why Gary Snodgrass, a senior vice president and chief administration officer at the energy services company Exelon, has developed a list of guidelines for meetings and reports. A big-picture manager who gets impatient with too much detail, Snodgrass gives the list to new hires to ensure that their presentations and written documents hit the mark, sparing everyone a lot of frustration. "My job is to guide them towards what I need so we're all more efficient and effective," he explains.

"I've worked for companies where senior management hired clones that are slightly less smart than themselves and therefore are unlikely to challenge them," says Christine Regan, CEO of Bone One Studios, an audio and video production company. "That always holds a company back. In today's ultracompetitive business environment, it's all about flawless execution. I liken it to being in a jazz band with each team member working off the other members' strengths and weaknesses, stepping forward solo to contribute where they are most able, and then coming back for a combined riff."

For Further Reading

When Sparks Fly: Igniting Creativity in Groups by Dorothy Leonard and Walter Swap (1999, Harvard Business School Press)

What Management Is: How It Works and Why It's Everyone's Business by Joan Magretta, with Nan Stone (2002, Free Press)

The Set-Up-to-Fail Syndrome: How Good Managers Cause Great People to Fail by Jean-François Manzoni and Jean-Louis Barsoux (2002, Harvard Business School Press)

Reprint U0210A

The Lessons of "Brand You"

Advice for Managing Talent

• • •

Kirsten D. Sandberg

In the irrational exuberance of the 1990s, management guru Tom Peters popularized the idea of turning a job search into a brand campaign. According to this "Brand You" theory, if you managed your career as though you were a premium brand with unique attributes and not just another commodity in a corporate cubicle, you'd get better work opportunities and higher pay in a job market where managers were scrambling to hire.

Now the labor market has shifted in employers' favor.

But that doesn't mean that the Brand You approach won't work; in fact, it could help both companies in their hiring and employees in the way they build and guide their own careers. At its best, the Brand You approach helps employers identify what a job seeker has to offer and what sets him apart from other job candidates. That can facilitate recruiting efforts, executive searches, and internal promotions.

Some managers, put off by all the self-promotion, worry that the Brand You mentality can have a divisive, destabilizing effect on an organization, says Laurence Prusak, executive director of the IBM Institute for Knowledge Management. Because they can be perceived as being only out for themselves, the Brand You achievers can end up causing trouble for the organization and for themselves, says Prusak: "Eventually, the organization exacts its revenge." Brand Yous can become organizational outcasts who can't move up so end up moving out.

But that's not to say that companies should shy away from hiring or promoting self-branded talents, Prusak continues. For one thing, few employees will ever become boardroom names like Tom Peters, let alone household names like Tiger Woods or Martha Stewart. But more important, a Brand You mindset is useful to the ongoing task of maximizing unit performance because it helps managers align employees with work they're passionate about.

Below, some advice about how the principles of branding apply to people.

Brand Yous Are Entrepreneurs, Not Just Marketers

Esteé Lauder and Michael Dell attained brand status by "comprehending consumers' emerging needs, developing a product that met these needs, communicating back and forth with customers, and actually delivering," thereby "making a market for novel goods and services," writes Nancy F. Koehn, professor of business administration at Harvard Business School and author of *Brand New*. "But they didn't wait around for some focus group to say, 'We need this!'" Peters adds. "They personally had an itch they needed to scratch," and in scratching it, they hit upon a highly marketable, ultimately brandable offering. They were exceptional business people, not just haughty hucksters.

Hiring people with this take-the-bull-by-the-horns personality for your team has some obvious benefits, but there are some important caveats, too:

Gauge how much entrepreneurial behavior your organization really needs.

Established Brand Yous will talk about what they can do for your company, based on what they've done for others. They're predictable and dependable, but their best innovations may be behind them. Aspiring Brand Yous will talk about what they hope to do for the company, based on how they've interpreted its needs. Although they are riskier hires, they present the possibility of greater unanticipated rewards, such as a solution to an organizational problem that managers haven't seen or the key to a customer's problem that market research hasn't revealed. The company can directly capitalize on, if not patent and brand separately, the employee's product or process innovation.

In your evaluation of candidates, emphasize performance over time.

A Brand You's résumé should convey real staying power, not just a string of successes. Moreover, genuine Brand Yous deliver steadfastly on their promises over time; they leave positions carefully, so as not to destroy what they've built (their brand equity).

Cultural Fit Is Critical

A company can admire an entrepreneur's achievements but despise her methods for achieving them. An individual's brand values should align with the overarching corporate umbrella brand, where the employee can operate naturally within the company's recognized and acceptable manner of business. Neal Lenarsky, founder and chairman of Strategic Transitions Inc. (STI), an executive management firm, tells the story of the head of programming at a major Hollywood studio. "He bounced from studio to studio, pushing through the same job over and over again, without ever asking himself, 'What's breaking down here? Why don't I belong anywhere?'" His managers failed to ask those questions as well.

As it turned out, his problem had nothing to do with his skill set and everything to do with a lack of aware-

> The Brand You concept can help managers frame staff development, as in "How can I manage this group of brands the way that a coach leverages various talents on a team?"

ness: neither he nor his managers really understood the kind of environment and the challenges he needed to thrive. The people hiring him accepted his experience at face value without probing to make sure there was a cultural fit.

In a flood of job applications, a Brand You identity

becomes a handy hiring filter—provided that the candidate's brand complements the company's culture. But if someone was born to be wild, identifies with Peter Fonda more than Peter Pan, and can see himself as an easy rider but not as a Mouseketeer, then chances are he belongs at Harley-Davidson, not at Walt Disney. Managers must articulate the set of behaviors that best characterize the desired culture of the corporate brand and discuss these during job interviews and performance reviews.

No Brand Is an Island

"Walt Disney could draw Mickey Mouse, but he still depended deeply on other cartoonists" to create full-length feature animations, says Prusak. The Brand You concept can help managers frame staff development, as in "How can I manage this group of brands the way that a coach leverages various talents on a team to optimize each one and to maximize the overall corporate brand?" Peters points to what Phil Jackson did at the Chicago Bulls: "Michael Jordan was just a record-setter until Jackson started coaching the Bulls." Once Jackson, a former professional basketball player himself, taught Jordan how to play on a team with other brand names such as Scottie Pippen under the Bulls' umbrella brand, Jordan started racking up championship rings and MVP titles.

As the manager, you've got to figure out how each

individual brand fits into the overall branded culture. Lead employees beyond the "Here's what Me Inc. can do for you" attitude; try to build cobranding partnerships instead. And reward people for positioning themselves relative to other brands on staff.

Extend the Brand with Great Caution

People can gain name recognition, says Lenarsky, by taking "an already existing brand to another level or to a broader audience," as Martha Stewart did. "She went from 'formidable banker' to 'media/magazine publisher' and has been extending her brand ever since." But when markets go south, managers are tempted to extend a brand by going down-market or mass-market, just to pay the bills.

One university dean assigned a famous professor to teach all four sections of an introductory course, each held at different times throughout the week. As a result, the professor's research and his reputation suffered. He lost a substantial grant, his teaching assistants and Ph.D. candidates complained about his office hours, and his students grew dissatisfied. Alternative ways to exploit the brand: Ask the star professor to coach junior staff members so that they can become better teachers. Team-teach so that the star needn't shine every week. Or design an electronic course for which the professor does everything once for the camera, to be broadcast live and recorded for later use.

Managers must work with employees to identify the core attributes of the brand before providing brand-extending opportunities. "Air Jordan" extended well into other basketball-related consumer brands like Nike shoes because Michael Jordan was the ultimate basketball athlete. But Jordan struggled to remake himself as a minor league baseball player and as an owner and manager of the Washington Wizards because his skill set didn't transfer. "Stretch goals" that extend beyond the job description can build expertise, brand awareness, and even customer loyalty without destroying the brand's core value. But if people find themselves enjoying their extension and neglecting what their constituents consider to be the core, then managers should consider launching a whole new brand—that is, a new way for that employee to create value under the corporate umbrella brand.

The bottom line: being a brand differs greatly from managing brands, but individuals and companies can both benefit from the Brand You approach. The key, says Prusak, is to recognize that "some people like working in large firms; some would rather be on their own. But both types are equally embedded in very strong networks of social, political, and economic reciprocities. No one's a standalone. We can't live that way. We'd be psychopaths." Figure out where each brand performs at its best relative to the others, and create a suite of work opportunities—full-time, part-time, and freelance—that allows you to manage each accordingly.

For Further Reading

In Good Company: How Social Capital Makes Organizations Work by Don Cohen and Laurence Prusak (2001, Harvard Business School Press)

Brand New: How Entrepreneurs Earned Consumers' Trust from Wedgwood to Dell by Nancy F. Koehn (2001, Harvard Business School Press)

The Brand You 50 (Reinventing Work): Fifty Ways to Transform Yourself from an "Employee" into a Brand That Shouts Distinction, Commitment, and Passion! by Tom Peters (1999, Knopf)

Reprint U0206C

Tap the Right Talent Pools

· · ·

The most successful companies tap the right talent pools—whether they're looking for leaders, contingent workers such as consultants, or new hires from a previously overlooked source (such as persons with disabilities). By knowing which talent sources to draw from and being willing to consider formerly under-represented employee populations, you widen your options significantly—thus boosting your chances of recruiting the best possible candidates.

In the following selections, you'll find helpful suggestions for developing exceptional leaders in your unit and evaluating internal and external candidates' leadership potential. You'll also discover that the best managers today know how to oversee large, fluid talent pools comprising contingent workers, consultants, and virtual teams. But finding these managers takes some creativity and ingenuity.

Evaluating, selecting, and working with consultants and previously untapped labor pools (such as disabled workers) also requires specific strategies. This section concludes with two articles that address these unique situations.

Do You Know What's in Your Leadership Pipeline?

• • •

Stephen J. Nelson

Some indicators in 2002 suggested that the U.S. economy was emerging from the doldrums. This was good news, of course, but it brought with it a hard realization for some companies looking to accelerate their growth plans: they didn't have the leadership talent they needed to do so.

In many corporations, strategic goals outstrip employees'

ability to deliver, says Dean Donovan, a vice president in the Johannesburg, South Africa, office of Bain & Company. The companies "simply don't have the people" to get from point A to point B. But the solution to this performance gap has less to do with hiring more or new people than it does with addressing an underlying leadership gap.

The job of a leader is to create alignment. Using the company's strategic goals as a framework, the leader tailors job responsibilities to take maximum advantage of employees' particular skills and abilities. So when a company is having difficulty meeting its overall performance targets, chances are that there's more tailoring that needs to be done—and that the leaders need to develop their tailoring skills.

Companies are accustomed to using gap analysis to identify key competitive weaknesses that need shoring up. But few companies think about applying gap-analysis techniques to their leadership-development issues. Donovan believes it's time to do precisely that.

Noel M. Tichy, professor of organizational behavior and human resource management at the University of Michigan's Graduate School of Business, agrees. "Most companies I work with need to rethink their leadership pipelines," he says. Back in the early '70s, the energy companies were known for forecasting their leadership needs 10 to 15 years down the road and developing their talent pool accordingly. "You'd be hard-pressed to find very many instances of exemplary pipeline development today."

But when business models can become obsolete within

a few months' time, is it even possible to anticipate leadership needs several years down the road? Yes, but only if you jettison the approach that prevailed two and three decades ago. You need to be more intentional about mapping your leadership skills to your strategic goals. You also need to accelerate the processes by which employees acquire the requisite abilities.

In addition, you need to emphasize a broader-based set of skills, says Tichy, who headed up General Electric's leadership training center, from 1985 to 1987. "Training leaders in strategic planning and operations management isn't enough anymore. In today's knowledge economy, the game is all about brains and alignment. You need people who are able to lead change and handle uncertainty, leaders with greater people acumen who are committed to helping their employees become smarter and to developing leadership skills in others."

Companies not only need to be more intentional and articulate about the leadership skills they require, they need to be more creative in designing experiences that help employees acquire them.

A Job That Starts, and Should Never Stop, with the Leader

Leadership pipeline development succeeds only when leaders—CEOs as well as division heads—make it a priority. Larry Bossidy, former CEO of AlliedSignal and now chairman of Honeywell, has built his reputation on leadership development. In his first couple of years at AlliedSignal, Bossidy writes in his book, *Execution: The Discipline of Getting Things Done,* he spent between 30% and 40% of his day "hiring, providing the right experiences for, and developing leaders."

Such tasks, Bossidy says, "simply cannot be delegated to others." The reason: as a leader, you must set the tone. You must know how your workforce stacks up against others in the industry. You need to ensure that candid appraisals occur throughout the company. Such evaluations must identify what employees do well and the areas in which they have to improve. You need to know "who is coaching your people, especially your good people," says Bossidy. And you're the one who must counteract the inertia caused by the failure to remove poor performers.

Moreover, when you're evaluating job candidates, it's not enough just to ask if a person is qualified for job A, you must also determine whether she can grow and be developed for job B, and then ask who you have, or will have, to refill job A. Your attention to these issues is vital because it will foster a leadership-development mindset that will cascade through the unit or organization.

Applying Gap-Analysis Thinking to the Leadership Pipeline

Talking the talk of pipeline development helps increase organizational awareness of the issue; conducting a thorough-going leadership gap analysis backs up the talk. To do this analysis, spell out the leadership needs that flow from each goal on your strategic plan. Then assess how your current leadership pool matches up with those needs and identify any deficiencies. As you move through the year, assess the leadership implications whenever a strategic goal is modified or a new one added.

Once the gaps have been identified, three issues become preeminent:

SUPPLY. What must you do to bring into the mix people with the skills you need to achieve your strategic goals?

DEPLOYMENT. "Many companies have sufficient talent," says Donovan, "but they just don't have it in the right places. If the core of the business is not achieving its full potential, these people need to be moved into the strategic core."

FULFILLMENT. What processes will you develop to ensure that people know what they are supposed to do and that they are motivated to do it?

One of Donovan's clients developed a five-year model of its talent pool, incorporating attrition rates and recruitment expectations. The resulting forecast: if the firm continued with business as usual, it would have 15% fewer managers than it needed to meet its strategic goals. Based on this analysis, the firm embarked upon some fairly typical plans for reducing attrition and improving the yield from its recruitment efforts. But more interestingly, it blended cross-training and change-management training into the mix. The goal here was not only to move personnel out of noncore businesses that had excess talent and into strategically critical businesses that had a talent shortage, but also to improve the organization's overall ability to seize upon fast-changing opportunities in dynamic markets.

"Human resources can facilitate this work," Donovan says, "but executive leadership must drive it." Not only should senior executives and unit leaders get involved in cross-checking performance data on key personnel, they should also make sure that the investments made in human resources are the ones that "can make the most difference."

Both "process and knowledge have evolved significantly in recent years," enabling companies to review their leadership needs in "much more sophisticated ways," says Donovan. For example, software that tracks key performance indicators makes it possible to monitor the initiatives that require stronger leadership and to "rank performance against objectives." The result: better management of the supply side of the leadership equation. Today executives can assess more carefully and critically the gap between "what they think they are going to generate in product, outcomes, or results, and what they will need in terms of personnel to do it," says Donovan.

Companies avoid hunting for leadership gaps at their peril, says Bossidy. "The tendency is to assume that you're fine—that you don't have any gaps. But the likelihood is that you do, so you must always be probing."

Productivity, Not Promise

One of the benefits of the gap-analysis process is that it forces you to articulate essential skills and attitudes for leadership in your company. That list of must-haves has definitely changed from 20 years ago, when leadership pipeline development was more prevalent in large corporations. Bossidy, for example, has come to focus more on employees' actual productivity than on their promise. Emphasize "people who are able to get things done, to execute," he says.

Similarly, Tom Grant, manager of executive development at Ford Motor Company, believes that "fast learners and doers" are more valuable than individuals who may prove unable to apply their gifts to the responsibilities and tasks at hand.

Ford's management-development system is evolving into one that encourages division heads and line managers to engage in a dialogue about leadership gaps. Regularly scheduled discussions enable all levels of leadership to get help thinking about the key positions under their supervision—what the individuals holding those positions are good at, what their professional desires and interests are, and who is being developed to replace them.

Real-Time Learning

Many solutions designed to address leadership gaps "are too elegant, and thus die of their own weight," says Susan Ennis, an executive-development consultant at Leadership Communications. An elaborate analytical system for identifying high-potential employees can become a roadblock, she cautions; it's far more important to give people stretch assignments. Tichy concurs. "Twenty percent of pipeline development involves leveraging formal development programs," he says. "Giving people the right work experience accounts for the other 80%."

The emphasis, in other words, is on real-time learning instead of classroom instruction. "The 21st century will be all about the teaching organization as opposed to the learning organization," says Tichy, author of the book *The Cycle of Leadership: How Great Leaders Teach Their Organizations to Win.* In a teaching organization, he explains, the learning doesn't happen as passively as it does in a learning organization. "Leaders at all levels of a teaching organization take responsibility for making their people and themselves smarter, as well as for training the next generation of leaders. There's more of an emphasis on action-learning, with CEOs and senior leaders being directly involved."

At the restaurant group Tricon Global, CEO David C. Novak personally teaches 10 three-day workshops a year. The Home Depot's Robert Nardelli expects his senior leaders to hold teach-ins right there on the store floor when they come across a significant new learning.

Says Tichy: "Leadership development is no longer something you can do offline. It has to be part of the everyday life of the company, woven into the very fabric of the organization."

Reprint U0205A

Which Schools of Experience Should Your Executives Attend?

• • •

Scott D. Anthony and Clayton M. Christensen

Everyone knows that companies seeking to create new-growth businesses must assemble the right management team. But how can you assess whether a company you are interested in has put the right team in place?

Consider two *Wall Street Journal* articles. One describes how San Francisco–based jeans maker Levi Strauss hired an executive from Houston-based motor-oil maker

Pennzoil to help the company successfully sell jeans to retailing giant Wal-Mart.

The other piece describes a new air-taxi company. Named Pogo, the service was co-created by two entrepreneurs: Robert Crandall, former CEO of AMR (the parent of American Airlines), and Donald Burr, founder of the pioneering discount airline People Express.

Do either of these companies have the right managers in place, given their stated goals? A concept called *schools of experience* leads us to believe that Levi Strauss has it absolutely right but that the air-taxi provider just might have it wrong.

Look to the Past, Predict the Future

University of Southern California business professor Morgan W. McCall Jr. introduced the concept of schools of experience in his 1998 book, *High Flyers: Developing the Next Generation of Leaders*. Its basic notion states that managers develop skills as they wrestle with the day-to-day challenges they face in their jobs. In other words, talented managers are molded rather than born.

Therefore, if you want to predict whether a particular manager will successfully tackle a specific challenge, you need to assess whether that manager attended the right schools of experience—that is, whether the individual's previous positions exposed him to experiences and taught him strategies that would help address his newest set of challenges.

A manager who has never faced a particular challenge might rise to the occasion, of course, but could just as easily default to previously successful strategies that would not necessarily work in the new context.

The schools-of-experience concept highlights two mistakes made by companies seeking to hire for innovation-

> ## Too much industry expertise could actually be a bad thing.

driven growth. The first error is to place too much emphasis on industry experience. The second is to hire an outsider blindly, without first considering whether anyone from within the company might already have the necessary experience.

Industry Experience Can Be Overrated

When a company seeks to crack into a new industry, advisers often will emphasize that the firm must have deep industry expertise to succeed. Depending on the situation, that advice could well be right—but it could also be wrong. If the company is hoping to shake up an established industry using a disruptive business model, too much industry expertise could actually be a bad thing.

"Deep expertise" means that when managers face common industry challenges, they will default to common industry solutions. When a company is bent on driving change, however, it needs to rely on new solutions and new strategies.

Consider Burr and Crandall's creation. Of course, the pair knows the airline industry inside and out. But if their goal is to disrupt the industry, they are both missing important schools of experience that might inhibit their ability to succeed.

Crandall and Burr—along with Burr's son, Cameron—have raised approximately $6 million in venture capital funding to build a business based on flying on-demand, short-haul, point-to-point routes using microjets. Priced competitively with first-class tickets, the service therefore will be significantly less expensive than chartering a jet.

Defining the Best Path to Disruption

Emerging air-taxi providers certainly have the potential to disrupt current industry leaders if they play their cards right. The best path to success (as is the case for all would-be disruptors) is to seek out nonconsumers: those without the skills or wealth to fly point-to-point routes. For example, a provider could target companies with suppliers in remote locations that are difficult to reach using existing services.

We worry that Burr's and Crandall's schools of experience will lead them to do just the opposite—i.e., to compete against consumption by providing an alternative to the airlines' most important short routes, such as the one between Boston and New York City.

This approach might work, but it is quite likely to incur a competitive response from leading airlines.

> When a company is bent on driving change, it needs to rely on new solutions and new strategies.

In short, their schools of experience could point Burr and Crandall into some version of the "compete against consumption" model instead of the "find people who aren't consuming" model.

The second mistake, hiring an outsider without thinking about what type of outside knowledge is required, results from classifying the world the wrong way. According to the schools-of-experience model, it is wrong to categorize would-be managers as either "insiders" or "outsiders." Being an outsider has little meaning if the candidate does not fill an important schools-of-experience gap on the management team.

It is better to categorize would-be managers as either "having attended the right schools of experience" or "having not attended the right schools of experience."

Whether a candidate comes from inside the organization or outside the organization is immaterial; what does matter is whether that candidate has wrestled with the sorts of challenges the new venture is sure to face.

Wal-Mart Experience Beats Industry Know-How

This is why it made sense for Levi Strauss to hire sales executive Ted Fox away from Pennzoil. The apparel manufacturer is going through a tough change as the balance of power shifts from consumer-goods manufacturers to mass-market retailers.

For a long time, Levi Strauss has sought to fight the rise of discount retailing, selling its goods through relatively high-end stores at premium prices. Levi Strauss's sales have dropped by approximately 40% during the past six years, however, and it has become clear that the company needs to sell through Wal-Mart and other discounters to survive.

But working with Wal-Mart presents an entirely new set of challenges compared with those that most of Levi Strauss's managers have faced. To begin with, Levi Strauss has to design its distribution model to fit Wal-Mart's low-price, high-turnover model; it has to find a way to make money on lower-priced products; and it has to feel comfortable working as a follower, not a leader.

Levi Strauss wisely sought to attract someone from a company that has a long history of dealing with these kinds of challenges. Fox's lack of knowledge about the apparel business was irrelevant. Because he had solved challenges related to working with Wal-Mart, he would increase Levi Strauss's chances of making this tough transition.

Although Levi Strauss initially struggled to change its business model, signs such as a 10% surge in sales in the first quarter of this year suggest it is finding success.

Other companies can similarly increase their chances of success by basing their hiring decisions on filling the gaps between the challenges they know they will face and the schools of experience their team has already attended.

For Further Reading

"Disruption Spreads Its Wings," *Seeing What's Next: Using the Theories of Innovation to Predict Industry Changes* by Clayton M. Christensen, Scott D. Anthony, and Erik A. Roth (2004, Harvard Business School Press)

High Flyers: Developing the Next Generation of Leaders by Morgan W. McCall Jr. (1998, Harvard Business School Press)

"Taxi! Fly Me to Cleveland" by Scott McCartney (*Wall Street Journal,* May 19, 2004)

"In Bow to Retailers' New Clout, Levi Strauss Makes Alterations" (*Wall Street Journal,* June 17, 2004)

Reprint U0411D

The War for Managerial Talent

. . .

Five-figure signing bonuses, desk-side manicures, free BMWs—these were the glitzy symbols of the corporate recruiting scene last year. A scarcity of top-notch professional talent, combined with a fast-growing economy and a fair amount of media hype, compelled many companies to offer anything and everything to potential candidates just to get them to sign on.

But that was last year. Since then, the picture has shifted somewhat. Companies are a little less frenzied in their pursuit of candidates, and there's certainly less pressure to offer boffo compensation packages. Even so, the power still resides with the employee, not the employer. People are more mobile, the labor market is more efficient, and job candidates have more options than ever before. Most important, the need for highly skilled people remains at an all-time high.

The solution? Create a strong leadership core, and rely on a large, fluid, and flexible talent pool to get the work done. This represents a new paradigm, one that requires a major shift in how you think about your workforce—and your job. Companies that fail to recognize this shift, caution the recruiting experts we spoke with, will become casualties in the war for talent.

Staffing the Work, Not the Jobs

In periods of rapid change, the news isn't always good, says Bruce Tulgan, president of RainmakerThinking and author of *Winning the Talent Wars*. "What defines the free market for talent is ups and downs, rapidly emerging market opportunities, and just as quickly disappearing market opportunities. The real challenge, when it comes to recruiting, is staffing up exactly as much as you need to, exactly in the skill areas where you need to, and remaining lean everywhere else."

The waves of downsizing, restructuring, and reengineering that occurred in the early 1990s signaled the end of the long-term model of employment. But as the economy began to improve, companies started to think that being lean wasn't so important. That was a mistake, says Tulgan. "Companies need to be lean and flexible. And that means focusing on retaining a strong core group.

You don't have to worry if your core group is getting smaller and smaller, as long as your fluid talent pool is getting bigger and bigger, and as long as you have the skills and systems to manage a fluid talent pool."

Many employers already have a fluid talent pool: they outsource, they use temp agencies, and they bring in consultants—all on an as-needed basis. But they need to do a better job of managing these pools, says Tulgan, listing two recommendations:

MAKE SURE THAT YOUR TALENT POOL IS WIDE AND DEEP. After all, the first person you call to take on a project may not be available right when you need him.

DEVELOP A SYSTEM FOR ORGANIZING TALENT ACCORD-ING TO SKILL AND PERFORMANCE ABILITY. Start out with the assumption that you're hiring a person to complete a particular piece of work. After all, very few people these days see themselves as long-term employees of a company—and those who do may work part-time, telecommute, work flexible hours, or take a year's sabbatical and then come back. But since these people aren't necessarily sitting in the office next door all the time, you need new ways of keeping track of them. Create a database that contains detailed information about occasional or potential workers' skills, track record, and contact information. Then, when projects need additional staff, you can fill the gaps using these external sources. An excellent, though often overlooked, way of building this talent pool is to keep track of outstanding former employees. Instead of letting people leave the company altogether, advises Tulgan, "put them in a reserve army, and call them back when you need them."

Wanted: A New Kind of Manager

Today's fluid talent pool puts new pressures on managers. It's a much greater challenge to create a high-performing unit out of part-timers, flex-timers, and virtual employees—as highly skilled as they may be—than it is with a workforce of full-time employees, all of whom are located in the same place. Not all managers can cope with the accompanying diversity and uncertainty. Exacerbating the problem is the fact that the prime pool of managerial candidates entering executive ranks (the number of people age 35–44) is expected to decline 15% over the next 15 years.

So how do you find managers who are up to these new challenges? *War for Talent 2000,* a recent study by McKinsey & Co., suggests that the answer may not lie in your formal recruiting process. According to Helen Handfield-Jones, a coauthor of this study of 56 companies, what separated the high-performing firms from the low-performing ones was the *attitude* toward recruiting. Leaders in the high-performing companies took recruitment personally. In concrete terms, says Handfield-

Jones, that means "taking the time to get deeply involved in people decisions and setting the involvement standard for others in the company." Some additional advice for how to pull this off:

Hunt for Talent All the Time

You always want to have talented people in the pipeline, says Tulgan. "We are seeing a lot of managers who are constantly recruiting—they have a number of people who have gone through the recruiting process at any given time, so they can hire much more quickly." Handfield-Jones agrees: "The process needs to be more talent-centric than position-centric."

Conduct Broader, More Imaginative Searches

"You used to be able to go to the same five schools, or you recruited only people from the same industry," says Handfield-Jones. "But today these pools are over-tapped—you're not going to find enough of the right kind of people if you limit yourself to a small number of traditional sources." Break out of the traditional mold by looking for people who have different educational backgrounds and who hail from different industries and countries. Similarly, don't get caught in the traditional trap of waiting for active job seekers to find you—these days, you need to do the hunting.

It's no surprise that the Internet can be an invaluable

tool here: some 2.5 million résumés are posted on an estimated 100,000 job-related sites across the Web. But if you're looking for the more hidden sources of managerial talent, firms such as Advanced Internet Recruiting Strategies can teach you how to locate pages on a company's Web site that can't be accessed through the home page. Containing a company directory, or the names of people working on a hot new project, such pages can be a gold mine.

Treat Job Candidates Like Customers

Today's hiring process, writes Peter Cappelli in the *Harvard Business Review*, is virtually indistinguishable from the marketing process. "Job candidates today need to be approached in much the same way as prospective customers: carefully identified and targeted, attracted to the company and its brand, and then sold on the job." From the first contact to the offer, the process must be fast and pleasant. In addition to screening and ensuring a good fit—the traditional hiring tasks—you need to be selling every step of the way. And just as you would go a long way to keep one of your most loyal customers, you need to be willing to bend your compensation policies, if necessary, to attract managers capable of wringing extraordinary performance out of a constantly shifting workforce.

"In the information age, talent is critical to value creation, and great talent has a much bigger impact than even average talent," says Handfield-Jones. The deep structural forces that are causing this war for talent will only grow stronger over the next 10 to 20 years. And the conditions that have created today's fluid talent pool will also remain for the foreseeable future.

In short, it's never been more important to have good talent, but managing good talent has never been more complicated. Which is why *finding* the right people to manage that talent has never been more crucial.

For Further Reading

Winning the Talent Wars by Bruce Tulgan (2001, W. W. Norton & Company)

"Making the Most of On-Line Recruiting" by Peter Cappelli (*Harvard Business Review,* March 2001)

Reprint U0103B

How to Choose — and Work with — Consultants

• • •

Tom Rodenhauser

The book *Dangerous Company* caused an uproar last year by vilifying the shoddy advice occasionally provided by some of the premier consulting firms—Boston Consulting Group and The Monitor Company, to name a couple. This is hardly surprising: the relatively secretive world of management consulting, unused to such public scrutiny, can be thin-skinned at times. Even though authors James O'Shea and Charles Madigan do tend toward the sensational, focusing on examples of soured consulting relationships that ended up in court, their account nevertheless underscores the importance of the maxim *Let the buyer beware* when it comes to selecting and collaborating with consultants.

What types of projects are best suited to outside consultants? How do you choose the most compatible consultant or firm? What level of service should you expect? And what are the keys to managing the relationship? Harvard Management Update offers the following primer on collaborating effectively with consultants.

When to Hire a Consultant

Generally, there are two reasons for hiring a consulting firm. One, there is a specific problem that needs addressing—an antiquated bill-processing system needs to be overhauled—and you lack the internal expertise. Two, you are considering a strategic business issue—your company is thinking about expanding into Europe—and require outside, objective counsel. Consultants are, first and foremost, advisors. Their advice is no substitute for certain preliminary work that only you (or your company) can carry out. So, before considering hiring a consultant, ask yourself four questions.

Do you have a clear understanding of the project's mission?

Clients and consultants often have different views of the ultimate goal, and the objectives are often vaguely defined (e.g., "improving a business process"). A consulting assignment without measurable targets usually results in disappointment. Before contacting consultants, spell out the scope and purpose of the proposed project.

Does management fully support—organizationally and financially—the consultant's mission?

The disengagement of senior management from the consulting project guarantees failure. All too often, front-line managers advocate consulting services without the full support of higher-ups. Conversely, senior executives may foist their favorite consultants upon unsuspecting managers. The internal disconnect wastes time and money and breeds distrust that poisons the project. Reach consensus on the need for outside counsel before going forward.

When should the engagement end?

Consulting and outsourcing are two vastly different activities. Business process management, as outsourcing is euphemistically called, is a long-term contract between the company and an outside agent to handle a central business operation. Consulting assignments should have a definite beginning and end. It's unwise and ultimately unprofitable to hire management consultants to run the entire business, which is what happens with open-ended engagements.

Can your company provide the necessary ongoing support after the project's completion?

Consulting is like exercise: without dedicated follow-up, it's wasted effort. To ensure continued success, monitor the post-consulting program closely.

Finding the Right Consultant

This can be a daunting task for those unfamiliar with the industry. Some database and directory companies, such as Dun & Bradstreet and Gale Research, identify more than 200,000 U.S. consulting firms. An equal number can be found in Europe and Asia. These sources can be helpful in pinpointing consulting firms by the industries they serve, their geographic location, or the services they provide. Most large consultancies have offices in every major city and are thus easy to contact. Increasingly, smaller firms are advertising their services via Web sites or through such brokering services as The Expert Marketplace or the Management Consultant Network.

Proposals

Once you've identified several likely candidates, request proposals from them. Consider proposals as the consultant's calling card. Never, under any circumstances, pay for a proposal or agree to a "handshake deal" for consulting services. And although there is no set formula for proposals, a well-crafted document will clearly and concisely answer the following:

- Does the consultant understand the problem?

- Are the approach and methodology for solving the problem clearly and succinctly presented?

- Are the benefits quantifiable?

- What are the consulting team's qualifications and experience?

- What are the fees?

Studying the proposal will give you a good feel for the firm's fit with your company. Jargon-filled proposals that don't define the end product are useless, says Tony Apante of CSC Consulting Group. "Clients need to clearly understand what results will be delivered and by when."

Consultants rarely describe the specifics of their work to outsiders for fear of breaching client confidentiality. This makes in-depth reference checking difficult—but it is vital nonetheless. Ask finalists for the names and numbers of clients whose projects most closely match your own.

Fees

After client engagements, fees rank as the most sensitive subject among consultants. Most consulting services are billed on a per-diem basis; retainers are used for long-term projects. The fees may seem exorbitant on the surface, but good consulting is worth the price, particularly when results are clearly defined. "Establishing clear measurement criteria takes time," says Marsha Lewin, a anagement consultant. "But the process allows the consultant and client to establish the standards for performance. The financial relationship is particularly important so that the client can attach dollar values to the benefits she'll get from the assignment, while the consultant knows what she'll receive for the work involved."

How to Guarantee Success

Consulting is still a personal service delivered by individuals. Since referrals speak to a firm's culture, they are probably the most reliable indicators of a consultancy's fit with your company and its specific needs. "Select a consultant based on personal fit with the organization," says Douglas Ferguson, a partner with Planning Technology Group. "A good client-consultant relationship is ultimately trust-based, where the consultant works hard to have an impact on an organization over time. If there

Questions to Ask Before Signing Up a Consulting Firm

What kinds of assignments has the firm conducted that are applicable to your problem? Consultants are experts at translating best practices across a broad variety of businesses. Still, you're generally better served by selecting firms with a successful track record in dealing with the issues your company is facing.

What is the firm's general reputation in the business community, particularly in your industry? One of the biggest critiques of consulting firms is that they send legions of MBAs to learn the client's industry. Outside perspective is fundamental to the consulting process, but hiring consultants unfamiliar with your industry can be dangerous.

Who is the lead consultant or project leader, and what is his or her background and experience? Consulting firms have a reputation for pulling the infamous "bait and switch" on clients: impressive partners with impeccable credentials dazzle clients into signing contracts, then junior consultants show up for the engagement.

What are the backgrounds of the other members of the consulting team? Consulting is a leveraged business: junior team members will do most of the analytical work under the direction of senior partners. Getting to know the junior team members builds trust and confidence.

What specific measurements of value added does the firm employ for each assignment? Strategy consultants generally use softer client-satisfaction techniques (client surveys) than operations-oriented consultants, who often fix fees against specific improvement benchmarks. Increasingly, consultants are considering an equity stake in a client's business as a form of payment, looking to increase the value of that equity through their efforts.

Can the firm provide a detailed breakdown of fees, including all costs of team members as well as clerical and out-of-pocket expenses? Larger firms deal with more overhead and so need to allocate those expenses throughout all their consulting engagements. Still, clients should have a clear understanding of fees and how they correlate to specific services.

Does the firm guarantee its work? Most consulting firms will work to the client's satisfaction, but rarely do they offer a 100% money-back guarantee. During the proposal phase, make sure that consultants specify their deliverables as precisely as possible.

Does the firm conduct a post-engagement analysis? Some consultants insist on a post-mortem for every assignment. This is the sign of a quality firm: such firms clearly have an interest in providing superior service.

What will be the operational impact of this consulting assignment on your company? Consultants should help you *reinvent* your business. You don't need help to achieve operational gains of 10%—steer clear of any consultant promising only such marginal gains.

is not a good personal fit, trust and impact are less likely." Moreover, many consulting assignments fail when clients abdicate their responsibility for managing the relationship. Consulting firms always assign a project leader to direct their team—clients should do likewise.

Ninety percent of all consulting assignments would never find their way into the pages of *Dangerous Company,* because they are successful. Still, consultants are not miracle workers, and clients aren't helpless—each is responsible for ensuring that the engagement achieves the desired results. When one side or the other fails to live up to that covenant, both are to blame.

***

For Further Reading

Harvard Business School 1999 Career Guide: Management Consulting edited by L. Neil Hunn (1998, Harvard Business School Press)

Consultants and Consulting Organizations Directory, 1999 19th Edition (1998, Gale Research)

Dangerous Company: Management Consultants and the Businesses They Save and Ruin by James O'Shea and Charles Madigan (1998, Viking Penguin)

How to Select and Use Management Consultants (1994, Association of Management Consulting Firms)

Reprint U9809A

Hiring Crunch?
Here's an Untapped
Labor Pool

. . .

William C. Hargis, Jr.

An industrial laundry isn't the most glamorous place in the world to work. It smells like chemicals. It's hot. My plant has about 60 employees who sort and weigh dirty clothes, then wash, dry, press, and fold them. Finding people to fill these jobs in a town with a 2.3% unemployment rate has been one of my toughest challenges. What helped me was targeting a hiring pool that not many managers think of—people with disabilities.

The plant I run, in Colonial Heights, Va., used to be

one of the lowest-paying in our company. Today our rates are competitive, but when I came there in 1998 we paid $5.45 an hour while other area employers were offering $6.30 for unskilled labor. Turnover was at 360%.

I placed employment ads in the local newspapers, which attracted a call from an administrator at a program called Greater Richmond Employment Assistance Team. He asked, "Have you ever thought about hiring people with disabilities?" He told me that the Virginia Department of Rehabilitative Services hosts monthly meetings for city, state, and county agencies where industry representatives can talk about jobs at their businesses. I said, "Get me in front of them," and he did. The response was good, and I began asking caseworkers and job candidates to come to the plant for a tour so they could learn about the positions and functions. After the tour, I'd ask the candidates what they thought they could do.

At first, my managers thought I was crazy to add more people to the payroll, especially people who might not work full time. I told them about the federal tax incentives that companies qualify for once someone with disabilities works 400 hours. Thanks to the incentives, I could essentially hire two people for one salary. That's how I sold it—but honestly I was just desperate to get people in here willing to do the job.

Right off the bat I hired a man in a wheelchair. He is physically impaired from the neck down and has limited hand mobility. He felt that he could work back in the soil dock, counting and weighing soiled towels.

His caseworker made sure he got here and worked beside him for several weeks. His station is a table surrounded by big laundry slings that are held open on carts. At first the sling carts were too high; he had to reach up and was getting tired. Then our maintenance guys built a ramp to elevate him. Now he could throw the towels down to the slings.

When he finished a task, he'd come to me or the plant manager and say, "I need something to do." We'd say, "Well, what else can you do?" He'd say, "That over there, I think I can do that." So now he knows three or four different areas. One of his jobs, for instance, is sorting hangers. Hangers usually come back to us in one big useless tangle. Nobody had the patience to sort them, so we'd throw them away—even though they cost four cents each. Now we save thousands of dollars each month on reused hangers.

Another of our wheelchair-bound employees is fairly mobile from the waist up. He works with a barcode scanner to sort clothes into bins, perfect for someone in a seated position. We've hired six people with disabilities so far. Two have been here over a year, a long time for my plant. They're never late. They work hard. That has really improved our morale.

Now I get a lot of calls from agencies. Our latest venture is with a nearby county agency called Chesterfield Employment Services (CES). They've offered to bring in five to eight fulltime employees with disabilities to fold towels. We'll pay them on a per-towel basis. CES will provide a manager and pay for their benefits.

We can't hire everyone who applies. One candidate, for example—a woman with a hearing disability—couldn't coordinate schedules with her agency-provided translator.

In the two years I've been running this plant, I've tried everything—prison labor, welfare-to-work, recruiting at local churches, pushing the city to put in a transit line near my plant. Hiring people with disabilities has made the most difference in our stability and morale. It's rewarding in a lot of ways—especially just to see something finally work.

Reprint U0008D

Use the Internet to Recruit

. . .

Today's hiring managers are using the Internet to recruit, screen, and hire talent—in addition to traditional methods such as search firms and asking current employees for referrals. But even while the Internet vastly increases your pool of candidates, it also raises unique challenges.

The articles in this section show you how to make the most of online recruiting and hiring—including strategies for using your company's Web site to attract qualified prospective employees. You'll also find suggestions for exploring unconventional approaches to Internet recruiting—such as finding candidates and leads in online discussion forums related to the expertise you're seeking.

Online Hiring?
Do It Right

• • •

Online recruitment is booming. The number of résumés posted on the Internet grew from 100,000 in 1995 to 2.5 million in 1998. Over the same period of time, the number of World Wide Web sites containing job listings exploded from 500 to 20,000, according to recruiting consulting firm Internet Business Network.

Where potential employees flock, companies follow. About 2,000 employers offer an average of 35,000 jobs at any one time on Careers.wsj.com, a job-placement site owned by the *Wall Street Journal* that ranks among the top three in the country. By 2003, estimates Forrester Research, 124,000 firms will be recruiting online. If your company is among those already recruiting on the Internet, pat yourself on the back: you're ahead of the curve.

Or are you? "When I go out to companies and say, 'Are you using the Internet to recruit?' the vast majority say yes. But then when I ask what it is they're doing, the answer is, 'Oh, we post some jobs on Monster.com' or 'We run ads in all these Sunday papers and the ads also appear online on our site.' That's not really using online recruiting," says Tony Lee, Careers.wsj.com's editor-in-chief and general manager.

Companies that use the Internet solely as an extension of paper-based recruiting practices are failing to exploit the power of the new medium. The Web allows managers to reach larger numbers of potential candidates, in venues that weren't available in the past. It also allows companies to pinpoint their recruiting efforts, and to set themselves apart from competitors through creative electronic tactics. The following are some tips—and some cautions.

Broaden the Pool of Candidates

In this drum-tight labor market, companies must use the Internet to reach both "active" and "passive" candidates, says Terry Williams, a high-tech recruiting specialist who heads T. Williams Consulting. *Active* candidates are those posting their résumés on online job boards. *Passive* candidates—well-qualified workers happily employed elsewhere—make up a larger and more appealing labor pool. "Yet I'd say that 90 to 95 percent of all high-tech companies fail to create a proactive sourcing strategy utilizing the Web," Williams says.

To reach passive candidates, Williams suggests dedicating a recruiting team solely to the task. "Set up a

> If your company is among those recruiting on the Internet, you're ahead of the curve. Or are you?

couple of people in HR and free them from customers—no résumés to process, no one to interview," he says. "Have them do demographic studies of the sorts of people you want to hire." Data in hand, the online recruiting team can then go to Web sites frequented by prime candidates.

If your company needs Java programmers, for instance, consider their probable age and preferences. Mostly between 22 and 29 years old, they surf the Web heavily. They're likely to visit several sites for information on Java—JavaWorld.com, *Java Developer's Journal* (www.java developersjournal.com/java), and Gamelan.com. They might check CMPnet.com for technology news, CNet.com for technology reviews, Tunes.com for music downloads and purchases, ESPN.com for sports, and CNN.com for news. Every one of these URLs accepts banner advertisements—but not many companies are advertising job openings there.

Home in on the Best Sources

Even in the dot-com age, some companies still fail to mention job openings or application procedures anywhere on their own Web sites. (An example: The Coca-Cola Co.) "It really boils down to the technical sophistication of companies," Lee says. "A lot of companies out there are struggling to make the best use of the Internet for recruiting. It's not an easy thing to do."

One lesson you'll learn early: *only* posting job openings on your company Web site or on big commercial boards, such as Monster.com, CareerMosaic.com, or Career-Path.com, is unlikely to yield the right candidates quickly enough—or at all. "These large databases are like an ocean," says Williams. One way to boost your odds is to target a smaller pond. An increasing number of Web sites focus on specific types of jobs in specific locales. Careers.wsj.com, for example, positions itself as the number-one site for mid- to senior-level executives.

For technical personnel, there's another feature of the Internet that's useful but often overlooked: Usenet. Usenet is a global system of discussion groups that runs parallel to the Internet, and its bulletin boards can be extremely specific on job function and location. For example, <fl.jobs.computers.programming> lists only job openings in Florida for computer programmers. A moderator even ensures that job postings meet site criteria. For high-tech firms in particular, another advantage of listing jobs on Usenet is their historic appeal to the digerati. "Any moron who knows how to use a browser can get to your Web site," observes Logan Roots, engineering manager of digital graphics firm Enroute Imaging, "but getting on Usenet takes some expertise." (Not as much as it used to, however. Web-based companies such as Intellinews.com provide user-friendly entry for a fee.)

Set Yourself Apart

Employers are coming up with clever uses of the Internet to differentiate themselves from competitors. Some companies link Datamasters.com and Relonetworks.com directly to their Web sites, thereby allowing potential applicants in other regions to compare costs of living and to estimate relocation costs. Others sport résumé builders on their Web sites. Caterpillar displays a fill-in-the-blank form on its site (www.cat.com) that encourages applicants to file on the spot rather than go through the drawn-out process of writing, printing, and mailing a résumé. The form also allows Cat to specify the information it wants from job-seekers, by inserting, for example, a field for "technical, manufacturing, or computer-based skills." Linked to the résumé-building

Keep Web Hiring in Perspective

With so many sites devoted to job-hunters' résumés or employers' openings, the Web is the place to turn when you're looking to hire, right?

Not necessarily. The low *quantity* and poor *quality* of recruiting information on the Web are the flip side of the current buzz over online hiring.

Quantity

Although 2.5 million résumés—the number said to be posted online today—sounds like a big number, it's a small fraction of the 140 million people in the American labor force. Market research firm Odyssey, in San Francisco, figures that only 12% of the 102 million households in the United States include anyone who has hunted for a job online. "The reason online recruiting is all you hear about is because the players in this field are buying Super Bowl ads," says Tony Lee of Careers.wsj.com. "People like to prognosticate about how things are going to change, and they point to the people who are building brands out there. But it's really no different than e-commerce; if you take a look at retail sales online, it's still just a very small percentage of all sales out there."

Online recruitment will surely grow, but right now most hiring action remains elsewhere. Forrester Research page is a regularly updated list of available positions at Cat, sorted by location, function, and division.

estimates that only 15,000 of all U.S. companies are currently recruiting online, with average spending per company only $7,000 a year.

Quality

As most people use it, the Web is unselective. Your job postings are available to all, regardless of qualifications or location. "The Web is a broadcast system," says Logan Roots, a manager at graphics firm Enroute Imaging. "You're casting a huge net, and who knows what you'll catch. Some of it's great, and some of it's lousy. There's no guarantee that Monster.com is going to get me anything but a lot of lost hours looking at résumés that don't fit."

The best source to find good people for your company, Roots believes, is the old-fashioned method: referrals from current employees. Terry Williams concurs: "Still the number-one source for stars is employee referrals. What you should use the Internet for is to boost that method." How? Williams recommends user-friendly posts of job openings on your company Web site—and then making sure current employees are kept up-to-date on hiring needs. Roots favors plain-vanilla e-mail. "Word of mouth is an e-mail thing, not a Web thing," he says. In Silicon Valley, "the world of computer engineers is small enough that if you get to know people, you can cover the ground. And the way you do that is by e-mail."

The prize for online-hiring creativity may go to DVCi Technologies, an IT marketing agency in New York City, which installed a Web camera in its offices last October for the benefit of potential recruits. Sited at www.recruitcam.com, the camera shows exactly how DVCi's offices look and how employees interact. "We have a really fun office and a great space," says SVP and account director Haim Ariav. "We thought, 'Why don't we try to leverage that?' I think a lot of these dot-com start-ups are working out of cubicles or temporary offices." The response has been gratifying, says Ariav: 40 to 50 individuals visit daily, on average, and both recent hires viewed the Webcam during negotiations with DVCi. "One of the reasons [our new designer] hired on was because of the recruitcam; she said it showed we were creative," Ariav says.

Webcams may or may not be for you—but if your company is a laggard, you need to get up to speed. "The recruiting game has become a marketing game," says Terry Williams. "You need to sell people on your company, and the way to do that is the Internet. The whole game has moved online."

Reprint U0002C

Finding Talent
on the Internet

. . .

Patricia Nakache

There's the rhetoric: People are our company's most
important asset. There's the old reality: The most important asset so long as we don't need to cut costs, in which
case we'll reluctantly part with 10% to 20% of our work
force. Then there's the new reality: Uhhh, maybe we cut
too deep—boy, is the job market tight, and if we're serious about this growth strategy, we're going to have to
find some smart, talented people, probably from the
outside. No wonder that the promise of recruiting better
people faster and cheaper through the Internet has be-
gun to intrigue the corporate world.

Thousands of companies are experimenting with electronic recruiting and a few on the leading edge have fully integrated it into their human resource strategy. The Good Guys!, a San Francisco-based electronics retailer, posts all its open positions on the Internet and now finds more than a third of its new hires through this medium. The Good Guys! and other pioneers have made an important discovery: A significant number of job-seekers log onto the Internet to look for opportunities—a survey by outplacement firm Drake Beam Morin puts the proportion at 19% of all job-seekers—and, not surprisingly given the demographics of Internet users, these job-seekers tend to be well qualified.

Practitioners of electronic recruiting agree that the Internet is most helpful for finding two types of job candidates: college students for entry-level and seasonal positions, and technical personnel, particularly those with hard-to-find skills. But the variety of positions posted on the Internet is broadening rapidly. On the Monster Board, one of the largest commercial job-listing services, non-technical job postings, including positions in healthcare, finance, sales, and marketing, have risen from 10% to 45% of all postings over the past three years. The salary range of the posted positions has widened commensurately, starting at $25,000 a year for entry-level administrative positions, up to the low six figures for senior managers and experienced engineers.

In short, companies aggressively engaged in electronic recruiting may be on their way to a distinct advantage in the global battle for intellectual capital. If your company hasn't yet started surfing the Net for its staffing needs, it's time to get started. Here's how:

Make the most of your company Web site

Nowadays, corporate Web sites are legion, but few are used to their full potential. In recruiting, your company Web site should be used not only to post job openings, but to market the company to prospective employees and to accept job applications. Eric Lane, Silicon Graphics' director of worldwide staffing, built the job opportunities section of his company's Web page with five design elements in mind: context (what the site is trying to accomplish), content, ease of navigation, functionality (what tools are provided for the user), and engagement (ways to attract users to the site). It's the last two elements that can truly set a Web site apart.

In terms of functionality, the Silicon Graphics Web site (www.sgi.com) offers a handy tool called the "résumé builder" to facilitate its job application process. It allows candidates to submit their résumés either by filling out an online form or by pasting into the form an existing electronic résumé file. These résumés are e-mailed to specific recruiters within Silicon Graphics if they match the requirements of existing job openings. They are also stored in a database for two years (or much longer for specific technical backgrounds) so that they can be considered for future openings. An added bonus for the job-seeker: The electronic résumé can also be submitted to other companies.

Building an engaging Web site, one that users might "bookmark" for easy future reference, is more art than science. Says Lane, "You need to add value to the interaction and make a good impression." For example, the College Connection section of the Silicon Graphics site lists not only questions that a candidate might be asked in an interview at Silicon Graphics, but also questions likely to be asked in interviews at Microsoft and Intel, along with possible responses. Students can add to the site questions they've been asked in the interviewing process. A cost-of-living adjustment tool allows students to compare the buying power of salaries in different cities.

So just how engaging is the Silicon Graphics site? Downright riveting, judging from its success. The company reports that it now finds 20% to 30% of new hires through the Internet, up from 5% only a year ago.

Experiment with commercial job-listing services

If the prospect of building a state-of-the-art Web site is overwhelming, or if you simply want to extend your reach to people who might not ordinarily visit your site, take a look at some of the Web's commercial job-listing services. A few providers, such as CareerMosaic (www. careermosaic.com) and The Monster Board (www.monster.com), dominate the industry. But there are literally

> ## Some companies now find a third of their new hires on the Net.

hundreds of others, including narrow niche services like showbizjobs.com (the name says it all) or coolworks.com (fun jobs, for example on cruise lines or at resorts) and electronic extensions of the job classifieds in trade and academic publications.

The economics of using a commercial job-listing service are compelling. In general, these services charge companies to list job openings but allow users to browse them for free. But while a print ad can cost hundreds of dollars for one weekend in a newspaper, CareerMosaic charges only $150 to list a job for 30 days. And the more jobs you post, the better the prices. For example, if you post more than 1,000 jobs with CareerMosaic, the price is $8 per listing. Teresa Toller, director of recruitment and staffing for The Good Guys!, reports that she receives on average 50 to 60 responses for every position that she posts. Even with far lower response rates, the cost per new hire through the Internet is likely to be lower than through other media.

From the large providers, companies can buy a number of services beyond plain vanilla job listings. These include employer profiles that are posted on the job-listing site and can serve as a company Web page substitute (only 50% of CareerMosaic customers have links to their own sites), banner advertising on the site's home page, "open houses" (packages consisting of banner advertising, company information, and job listings), and access to the provider's résumé banks.

If it's college students that you're after, you should check out JOBTRAK (www.jobtrak.com), a job-listing service for students and alumni at more than 500 colleges nationwide. To post jobs, employers pay a fee that is split between JOBTRAK and the colleges. Employers have the option to target their listings to a specific group of colleges such as the Ivy League. Students and subscribing alumni are given passwords to access the listings for their school.

Your company doesn't have to be technically sophisticated or even have Internet access to benefit from these services. Wolff Dinapoli, a franchisee of Hilton Hotels in southern California, has used JOBTRAK to fill 20 entry-level assistant manager positions, mostly with graduates of UCLA and USC. The company sends its job listings to JOBTRAK and receives applications by fax. Says Keith Wolff, general manager of Wolff Dinapoli, "We didn't sign up for JOBTRAK because it was online. It was more

the type of person it could help us recruit: college graduates with computer skills."

Identify the job-listing services that best meet your
needs, and evaluate them along the same five design criteria that Lane used to build the Silicon Graphics site. It
is difficult to compare the sizes and usage rates of different services because they typically use different measures. But be sure to ask what advertising they do to
attract users to their site, how many positions they have
posted, and how long positions remain posted. For
example, to attract users, The Monster Board runs ban-
ners on the major search engines, uses radio spots, and
has started to use outdoor advertising. Tellingly, major
newspapers, which profit from job classifieds, refuse to
run the service's advertisements.

Explore unconventional approaches to Internet recruiting

For urgent hiring needs or positions requiring specialized
skills, try some imaginative approaches to electronic
recruiting. For example, you can browse the Usenet—a
collection of electronic bulletin boards, often referred to
as the backroads of the Internet—to identify forums
related to the specific expertise you are seeking. The participants in the discussion could be potential candidates
or they may have good leads. Says Silicon Graphics'
Lane, "We may only recruit 5% of our new hires this way,

but our accuracy is extremely high." However, be sure to mind your cybermanners: To minimize commercial intrusions into the Net's open forums, only use this approach selectively.

You can also post listings on or create links from other Web sites that are frequently visited, particularly by the types of professionals you want to recruit. For example, to recruit temporary store help at Christmas time, The Good Guys! created a link from the well-advertised Web site of a local television station, KRON.

> Tellingly, newspapers refuse to run advertisements from an online job-listing service.

Alternatively, you can search through some of the Web's résumé banks, including those run by the commercial job listing services. The Monster Board has developed a search agent for employers called 'Cruiter that will continuously troll its résumé bank for candidates who meet your job requirements.

As yet, most companies do not look to fill executive-level positions through the Internet. Jon Carter, a partner with the executive search firm Egon Zehnder, cites three reasons. First, companies often don't want to advertise that they are looking to fill an executive post. Second, the type of people sought for executive positions are usually highly successful and tend not to be active job-seekers. Finally, these individuals want to be recruited in a personalized way, not through a computer.

Nevertheless, even for high-level jobs, the Internet can facilitate and accelerate the recruiting process. At the most basic level, résumés and correspondence can be mailed electronically. But in addition, search firms can rapidly identify companies that may offer a potential source of candidates and, conversely, candidates can quickly research prospective employers. Jon Carter describes an increasingly common scenario: "The moment I mention the name of my client to a potential candidate, right away he is pulling up information about the company faster than I can get my spiel out. He can quickly size up the company and tell me whether or not he's interested." With a more efficient access to greater amounts of information, candidates are also much better prepared for interviews.

What does the future hold for electronic recruiting? It will continue to grow dramatically, attracting more companies for an even broader mix of recruiting needs. Forrester Research projects that revenues of the electronic recruiting industry will double from $4 million in 1996 to $8 million in 1997, and will then explode to something like $52 million in 1998. Expect experimentation and progress along a number of fronts: more sophisticated search agents to match résumés with job requirements, use of the Internet for screening interviews, and personal Web pages.

As it has done with other markets, the Internet will fundamentally improve the efficiency of labor markets. But just as the growing use of fax machines did not herald the end of regular mail, neither will online recruiting replace print ads and search firms. Instead, smart companies will increasingly take a selective, targeted approach to recruiting, using each medium for what it does best.

Reprint U9704D

About the Contributors

Michael Hattersley is a contributor to *Harvard Management Update*.

Melissa Raffoni is president of Human Asset Development Company and ProfessionalSkills.com, in Boston. She specializes in organizational development, executive coaching, and management development.

Heather C. Liston is a contributor to *Harvard Management Update*.

David Stauffer is a contributor to *Harvard Management Update*.

Edward Prewitt is a contributor to *Harvard Management Update*.

Liz Simpson is the author of nine books, including *Working from the Heart: A Practical Guide to Loving What You Do for a Living*. (Random House, 1999).

Kirsten D. Sandberg is an executive editor at Harvard Business School Press and a contributor to *Harvard Management Update*.

Stephen J. Nelson is the author of *Leaders in the Crucible: The Moral Voice of College Presidents* (Bergin & Garvey, 2000).

About the Contributors

Scott D. Anthony is a partner at Innosight.

Clayton M. Christensen is Robert and Jane Cizik Professor of Business Administration at Harvard Business School and author of numerous books. He is also the coauthor with Michael E. Raynor, of *The Innovator's Solution: Creating and Sustaining Successful Growth* (HBS Press, 2003).

Tom Rodenhauser is a contributor to *Harvard Management Update*.

William C. Hargis, Jr. is a general manager for Coyne Textile Services, a national industrial laundry company based in Syracuse, NY.

Patricia Nakache is a contributor to *Harvard Management Update*.

Harvard Business Review Paperback Series

The Harvard Business Review Paperback Series offers the best thinking on cutting-edge management ideas from the world's leading thinkers, researchers, and managers. Designed for leaders who believe in the power of ideas to change business, these books will be useful to managers at all levels of experience, but especially senior executives and general managers. In addition, this series is widely used in training and executive development programs.

These books are priced at US$19.95
Price subject to change.

Title	Product #
Harvard Business Review **Interviews with CEOs**	3294
Harvard Business Review on **Advances in Strategy**	8032
Harvard Business Review on **Appraising Employee Performance**	7685
Harvard Business Review on **Becoming a High Performance Manager**	1296
Harvard Business Review on **Brand Management**	1445
Harvard Business Review on **Breakthrough Leadership**	8059
Harvard Business Review on **Breakthrough Thinking**	181X
Harvard Business Review on **Building Personal and Organizational Resilience**	2721
Harvard Business Review on **Business and the Environment**	2336
Harvard Business Review on **The Business Value of IT**	9121
Harvard Business Review on **Change**	8842
Harvard Business Review on **Compensation**	701X
Harvard Business Review on **Corporate Ethics**	273X
Harvard Business Review on **Corporate Governance**	2379
Harvard Business Review on **Corporate Responsibility**	2748
Harvard Business Review on **Corporate Strategy**	1429
Harvard Business Review on **Crisis Management**	2352
Harvard Business Review on **Culture and Change**	8369
Harvard Business Review on **Customer Relationship Management**	6994
Harvard Business Review on **Decision Making**	5572

Title	Product #
Harvard Business Review on **Developing Leaders**	5003
Harvard Business Review on **Doing Business in China**	6387
Harvard Business Review on **Effective Communication**	1437
Harvard Business Review on **Entrepreneurship**	9105
Harvard Business Review on **Finding and Keeping the Best People**	5564
Harvard Business Review on **Innovation**	6145
Harvard Business Review on **The Innovative Enterprise**	130X
Harvard Business Review on **Knowledge Management**	8818
Harvard Business Review on **Leadership**	8834
Harvard Business Review on **Leadership at the Top**	2756
Harvard Business Review on **Leadership in a Changed World**	5011
Harvard Business Review on **Leading in Turbulent Times**	1806
Harvard Business Review on **Managing Diversity**	7001
Harvard Business Review on **Managing High-Tech Industries**	1828
Harvard Business Review on **Managing People**	9075
Harvard Business Review on **Managing Projects**	6395
Harvard Business Review on **Managing the Value Chain**	2344
Harvard Business Review on **Managing Uncertainty**	9083
Harvard Business Review on **Managing Your Career**	1318
Harvard Business Review on **Marketing**	8040
Harvard Business Review on **Measuring Corporate Performance**	8826
Harvard Business Review on **Mergers and Acquisitions**	5556
Harvard Business Review on **Mind of the Leader**	6409
Harvard Business Review on **Motivating People**	1326
Harvard Business Review on **Negotiation**	2360
Harvard Business Review on **Nonprofits**	9091
Harvard Business Review on **Organizational Learning**	6153
Harvard Business Review on **Strategic Alliances**	1334
Harvard Business Review on **Strategies for Growth**	8850
Harvard Business Review on **Teams That Succeed**	502X
Harvard Business Review on **Turnarounds**	6366
Harvard Business Review on **What Makes a Leader**	6374
Harvard Business Review on **Work and Life Balance**	3286

To order, call 1-800-668-6780, or go online at www.HBSPress.org

Harvard Business Essentials

In the fast-paced world of business today, everyone needs a personal resource—a place to go for advice, coaching, background information, or answers. The Harvard Business Essentials series fits the bill. Concise and straightforward, these books provide highly practical advice for readers at all levels of experience. Whether you are a new manager interested in expanding your skills or an experienced executive looking to stay on top, these solution-oriented books give you the reliable tips and tools you need to improve your performance and get the job done. Harvard Business Essentials titles will quickly become your constant companions and trusted guides.

These books are priced at US$19.95, except as noted.
Price subject to change.

Title	Product #
Harvard Business Essentials: **Negotiation**	1113
Harvard Business Essentials: **Managing Creativity and Innovation**	1121
Harvard Business Essentials: **Managing Change and Transition**	8741
Harvard Business Essentials: **Hiring and Keeping the Best People**	875X
Harvard Business Essentials: **Finance for Managers**	8768
Harvard Business Essentials: **Business Communication**	113X
Harvard Business Essentials: **Manager's Toolkit ($24.95)**	2896
Harvard Business Essentials: **Managing Projects Large and Small**	3213
Harvard Business Essentials: **Creating Teams with an Edge**	290X
Harvard Business Essentials: **Entrepreneur's Toolkit**	4368
Harvard Business Essentials: **Coaching and Mentoring**	435X
Harvard Business Essentials: **Crisis Management**	4376
Harvard Business Essentials: **Time Management**	6336
Harvard Business Essentials: **Power, Influence, and Persuasion**	631X
Harvard Business Essentials: **Strategy**	6328

The Results-Driven Manager

The Results-Driven Manager series collects timely articles from *Harvard Management Update* and *Harvard Management Communication Letter* to help senior to middle managers sharpen their skills, increase their effectiveness, and gain a competitive edge. Presented in a concise, accessible format to save managers valuable time, these books offer authoritative insights and techniques for improving job performance and achieving immediate results.

These books are priced at US$14.95
Price subject to change.

Title	Product #
The Results-Driven Manager: **Face-to-Face Communications for Clarity and Impact**	3477
The Results-Driven Manager: **Managing Yourself for the Career You Want**	3469
The Results-Driven Manager: **Presentations That Persuade and Motivate**	3493
The Results-Driven Manager: **Teams That Click**	3507
The Results-Driven Manager: **Winning Negotiations That Preserve Relationships**	3485
The Results-Driven Manager: **Dealing with Difficult People**	6344
The Results-Driven Manager: **Taking Control of Your Time**	6352
The Results-Driven Manager: **Getting People on Board**	6360
The Results-Driven Manager: **Motivating People for Improved Performance**	7790
The Results-Driven Manager: **Becoming an Effective Leader**	7804
The Results-Driven Manager: **Managing Change to Reduce Resistance**	7812
The Results-Driven Manager: **Hiring Smart for Competitive Advantage**	9726
The Results-Driven Manager: **Retaining Your Best People**	9734
The Results-Driven Manager: **Business Etiquette for the New Workplace**	9742

To order, call 1-800-668-6780, or go online at www.HBSPress.org

Management Dilemmas:
Case Studies from the Pages of
Harvard Business Review

When facing a difficult management challenge, wouldn't it be great if you could turn to a panel of experts to help guide you to the right decision? Now you can, with books from the Management Dilemmas series. Drawn from the pages of *Harvard Business Review*, each insightful guide poses a range of familiar and perplexing business situations and shares the wisdom of a small group of leading experts on how each of them would resolve the problem. Engagingly written, these interactive, solutions-oriented collections allow readers to match wits with the experts. They are designed to help managers hone their instincts and problem-solving skills to make sound judgment calls on everyday management dilemmas.